Nice & Cannes

WHAT'S NEW | WHAT'S ON | WHAT'S BEST

timeout.com/travel

Contents

Published by Time Out Guides Ltd
Universal House
251 Tottenham Court Road
London W1T 7AB
Tel: + 44 (0)20 7813 3000
Fax: + 44 (0)20 7813 6001
Email: guides@timeout.com
www.timeout.com

Managing Director Peter Fiennes
Financial Director Gareth Garner
Editorial Director Ruth Jarvis
Deputy Series Editor Dominic Earle
Editorial Manager Holly Pick
Assistant Management Accountant Ija Krasnikova

Time Out Guides is a wholly owned subsidiary of Time Out Group Ltd.

© Time Out Group Ltd
Chairman Tony Elliott
Financial Director Richard Waterlow
Group General Manager/Director Nichola Coulthard
Time Out Magazine Ltd MD Richard Waterlow
Time Out Communications Ltd MD David Pepper
Time Out International MD Cathy Runciman
Production Director Mark Lamond
Group Marketing Director John Luck
Group Art Director John Oakey
Group IT Director Simon Chappell

Time Out and the Time Out logo are trademarks of Time Out Group Ltd.

This edition first published in Great Britain in 2008 by Ebury Publishing
A Random House Group Company
Company information can be found on www.randomhouse.co.uk
10 9 8 7 6 5 4 3 2 1

For further distribution details, see www.timeout.com

ISBN: 978-1-84670-080-4

A CIP catalogue record for this book is available from the British Library

Printed and bound by Firmengruppe APPL, aprinta druck, Wemding, Germany

The Random House Group Limited makes every effort to ensure that the papers used
in our books are made from trees that have been legally sourced from well-managed
and credibly certified forests. Our paper procurement policy can be found on
www.rbooks.co.uk/environment.

Nice & Cannes Shortlist

The **Time Out Nice & Cannes Shortlist** is one of a new series of guides that draws on Time Out's background as a magazine publisher to keep you current with what's going on in town. As well as key sights and the best eating, drinking and leisure options, the guide picks out the most exciting venues to have recently opened and gives a full calendar of annual events. It also includes features on the important news, trends and openings, all compiled by locally based editors and writers. Whether you're visiting for the first time, or you're a regular, you'll find the *Time Out Nice & Cannes Shortlist* contains all you need to know, in a portable and easy-to-use format.

The guide divides Nice into five areas, each of which contains listings for Sights & Museums, Eating & Drinking, Shopping, Nightlife and Arts & Leisure, with maps pinpointing their locations where possible. Cannes has its own chapter with the same range of listings as for Nice, each shown on the map of the town. At the front of the book are chapters rounding up these scenes city-wide, and giving a shortlist of our overall picks in a variety of categories. We include itineraries for days out, plus essentials such as transport information and hotels.

Our listings give phone numbers as dialled within France. The international code for France is 33. To call from outside France follow this with the number given, dropping the initial '0'. Some listed numbers (usually 06) are mobiles, indicated as such.

We have noted differing price categories by using one to four € signs (€-€€€€), representing budget, moderate, expensive and luxury. Major credit cards are accepted unless otherwise stated. We have also indicated when a venue is NEW.

All our listings are double-checked, but places do sometimes close or change their hours or prices, so it's a good idea to call a venue before visiting. While every effort has been made to ensure accuracy, the publishers cannot accept responsibility for any errors that this guide may contain.

Venues are marked on the maps using symbols numbered according to their order within the chapter and colour-coded according to the type of venue they represent:

❶ Sights & museums
❶ Eating & drinking
❶ Shopping
❶ Nightlife
❶ Arts & leisure
❶ Hotels

Map key

Major sight or landmark	
Railway stations	
Railway lines	
Parks	
Pedestrian zones	
Churches	✚
Steps	
Area name	VIEUX NICE

Time Out Nice & Cannes Shortlist

EDITORIAL
Editor Sam Le Quesne
Deputy Editor Edoardo Albert
Proofreader Patrick Mulkern

DESIGN
Art Director Scott Moore
Art Editor Pinelope Kourmouzoglou
Senior Designer Henry Elphick
Graphic Designer Gemma Doyle
Junior Graphic Designer Kei Ishimaru
Digital Imaging Simon Foster
Advertising Designer Jodi Sher
Picture Editor Jael Marschner
Deputy Picture Editor Katie Morris
Picture Researcher Helen McFarland
Picture Desk Assistant Troy Bailey

ADVERTISING
Sales Director/Sponsorship Mark Phillips
International Sales Manager
  Kasimir Berger
International Sales Consultant
  Ross Canadé
International Sales Executive
  Charlie Sokol
Advertising Sales (Nice & Cannes)
  Carlos Pineda
Advertising Assistant Kate Staddon

MARKETING
Marketing Manager Yvonne Poon
Sales & Marketing Director, North America Lisa Levinson
Marketing Designer Anthony Huggins

PRODUCTION
Production Manager Brendan McKeown
Production Controller Caroline Bradford

CONTRIBUTORS
This guide was researched and written by Sam Le Quesne.

PHOTOGRAPHY
All photography by Karl Blackwell, except: page 29, 31, 33, 132, 145 Office du Tourisme & des Congrès de Nice / Nice & You; page 44, 45, 128, 148 Sam Le Quesne; page 83 CANCA; page 115, 125, 128 SEMEC; page 140 www.hi-hotel.net.

Cover photograph: Seaside resort, Côte d'Azur, Credit: Giovanni Simeone/ 4Corners Images.

MAPS
JS Graphics (john@jsgraphics.co.uk).

Thanks to Rosa, Philippe, Petra and Karin.

About Time Out

Founded in 1968, Time Out has expanded from humble London beginnings into the leading resource for those wanting to know what's happening in the world's greatest cities. As well as our influential what's-on weeklies in London, New York and Chicago, we publish more than a dozen other listings magazines in cities as varied as Beijing and Mumbai. The magazines established Time Out's trademark style: sharp writing, informed reviewing and bang up-to-date inside knowledge of every scene.

Time Out made the natural leap into travel guides in the 1980s with the City Guide series, which now extends to over 50 destinations around the world. Written and researched by expert local writers and generously illustrated with original photography, the full-size guides cover a larger area than our Shortlist guides and include many more venue reviews, along with additional background features and a full set of maps.

Throughout this rapid growth, the company has remained proudly independent, still owned by Tony Elliott nearly four decades after he started Time Out London as a single fold-out sheet of A5 paper. This independence extends to the editorial content of all our publications, this Shortlist included. No establishment has been featured because it has advertised, and no payment has influenced any of our reviews. And, for our critics, there's definitely no such thing as a free lunch: all restaurants and bars are visited and reviewed anonymously, and Time Out always picks up the bill. For more about the company, see www.timeout.com.

Don't Miss

Place Masséna

Sights & Museums

After Paris Charles de Gaulle, Nice's airport is the busiest in France. It's scarcely possible to lie on the beach for more than ten minutes without seeing a plane arcing slowly over the bay towards the distant runways. And yet, with tourists shipping in from every corner of the globe, Nice remains remarkably unfazed by the attention. Resolutely itself, the city welcomes foreigners but unlike many of its counterparts up and down this stretch of coast, it doesn't pander to them. It hasn't lost its soul to the tourist dollar.

New public spaces

By far the most discussed, scrutinised, criticised and (now) pedestrianised space in Nice is the newly altered place Masséna (box p78). This giant square has finally been converted from a morass of ring roads, taxi ranks and messy bus stops into one large, open public space. Depending on your viewpoint, 'large' and 'open' can mean a welcome breath of fresh air or a tundra-like environment where shade, aesthetics and convenience have all been sacrificed at the altar of municipal meanness. Therein lies the ongoing debate. But the likelihood is that most people will form no particularly strong feeling either way about what is essentially an innocuous pedestrianised square. Except, perhaps, for its fountain (the source of a good many *oohs* and *aahs* from first-time visitors), it goes largely unnoticed by those who do not have to live on or near it.

Another large brushstroke to have altered the canvas of Nice's town centre is that of the all-new tramway. A vast amount of time, work and money have been poured into this project, which connects the city's remoter areas with the old and new towns via a two-pronged overland tramline. What's more, the stops and the routes themselves have been transformed into individual artworks thanks to an ongoing initiative to commission installations and sculptures from a number of European artists (p83).

Also new is the Palais Masséna's Musée d'Art et d'Histoire (p94), which was, at the time of writing, about to be reopened to the public after an extensive period of refurbishment and restoration work. For further information, drop in at the Centre du Patrimoine (p91), which also finds itself in spanking new premises in one of the quai des Etats-Unis' beautifully restored 19th-century *terrasses*. The Centre also runs a programme of excellent guided walks, which make good introductions to the city.

Now and then

There's a healthy mix of old and new in Nice when it comes to fine art. On the contemporary side, the unrivalled champion of the scene is the Musée d'Art Moderne et d'Art Contemporain (p71). Its large permanent collection features a good showing from the Nice School, New Realism and Pop Art, while some of the billings in the temporary galleries are world class in their scope (the recent Pistoletto retrospective being an example). Aside from the MAMAC, Vieux Nice's two smaller municipal galleries, Galerie du Château (p53) and near neighbour Galerie Jean Renoir (p53), do a good job of patrolling for talented newcomers.

SHORTLIST

Must-see modern art
- Galerie du Château (p53)
- Galerie Jean Renoir (p53)
- Musée d'Art et d'Histoire (p94)
- Théâtre de la Photographie et de l'Image (p71)
- Villa Arson (p113)

Best of the past
- Musée de Paléontologie Humaine de Terra Amata (p100)
- Musée des Beaux-Arts (p108)
- Musée International d'Art Naïf Anatole Jakovsky (p108)
- Palais Lascaris (p54)

Best big names
- Musée Matisse (p108)
- Musée National Message Biblique Marc Chagall (p111)

Best views
- L'Eglise et Le Monastère Notre Dame de Cimiez (p107)

Charming churches
- Cathédrale de Sainte Réparate (p49)
- Cathédrale Saint Nicolas (p107)
- Chapelle de la Miséricorde (p49)
- L'Eglise de l'Annonciation (p52)
- Prieuré du Vieux Logis (p111)

Architectural assets
- Musée des Arts Asiatiques (p108)
- Observatoire de Nice (p111)

Best free
- Chapelle de la Miséricorde (p49)
- Galerie du Château (p53)
- Palais Lascaris (p54)

DON'T MISS

Palais Lascaris p12

A short hop out of town, Villa Arson (p113) is a catch-all centre for contemporary art set in a rambling 18th-century villa. Under the aegis of the French culture ministry, Villa Arson is home to a renowned art school, the Centre National d'Art Contemporain, and of course, an exhibition space. Work on display tends to be more at the cutting edge of the contemporary art scene than anything you'll find in the MAMAC (as witnessed by a recent show featuring work by Turner Prize winner Jeremy Deller). In a different medium, but a similar vein, the Théâtre de la Photographie et de l'Image (p71) provides wall space to a good many burgeoning young talents of the modern photography and multimedia art worlds.

Looking back over the centuries, Nice has a few strongholds of international art and culture. The two most famous are the eponymous museums dedicated to Matisse and Chagall. The Musée Matisse (p108) houses a huge number of the artist's paintings,

drawings, engravings and personal effects in the serene surroundings of a 17th-century villa. By contrast, the Musée National Message Biblique Marc Chagall (p111) is anything but serene, with its collection of biblically themed paintings, whose delirious assault of colour and imagery are juxtaposed with the stark, bunker-like aesthetic of the museum itself.

It is perhaps best not to describe the Musée des Beaux-Arts (p108) as a stronghold of international art (it recently suffered the theft of four of its masterpieces; p112), but it is certainly a treasure trove. From 15th-century altar pieces to work by 18th-century greats like Fragonard and 19th-century titans of the Impressionist movement, the museum's collection is nothing if not wide-ranging. The palatial setting (the building is the former residence of a Ukrainian princess) and gorgeous gardens are added attractions. Also a short journey from the town centre is the Musée International d'Art Naïf Anatole Jakovsky (p108), whose exhaustive collection of this artistic movement contains some real little gems.

Painting a picture of life in Nice over the centuries is also a speciality of the city's museums. In the heart of Vieux Nice, Palais Lascaris (p54) is a 17th-century villa housing all kinds of vestiges of the intervening eras, from frescoes, statues and artworks to a comprehensive display of musical instruments and a spooky 18th-century apothecary. Reaching still further back through time, the immaculately presented Musée de Paléontologie Humaine de Terra Amata (p100) puts forward a vision of the prehistoric communities who lived in these parts. A reconstruction of an ancient encampment and sundry evidence of prehistoric life seek to answer the challenge emblazoned across one of the museum's walls: 'Where do we come from?'

Holier than thou

Some of the city's most splendid sights have been built out of faith and, fervent believer or unflinching atheist, most visitors will find something of exquisite beauty in the churches of Vieux Nice and beyond. The largest, and arguably the most significant of these is the Cathédrale de Sainte Réparate (p49), which numbers among its many attributes Genoese-style tiling on its dome, a triptych of valuable organs scattered around the interior and gloriously imposing statuary. Just a short walk away, although some stylistic distance from the cathedral, is the Chapelle de la Miséricorde (p49), which is considered one of the finest examples of Baroque religious architecture in France. Its ceiling frescoes alone are worth the trip, as is Jean Miralhet's 15th-century masterpiece *La Vierge de Miséricorde*. And, while not in

the same league as the Chapelle, the Baroque adornments of L'Eglise de l'Annonciation (p52) are also quite spectacular.

A short journey out of town, the Cathédrale Saint Nicolas (p107) or 'Russian Church' is one of the most arresting sights not only in Nice but on the whole of the Riviera. Its five brilliantly coloured onion-domed cupolas are one of the most striking examples of Russian Orthodox architecture outside of Russia itself. Also worth a look are the L'Eglise et Le Monastère Notre Dame de Cimiez (p107), not least for the monastery's gorgeous, panoramic gardens, and the Prieuré du Vieux Logis (p111), which is a heaven on earth for fans of religious art.

Neighbourhoods

Not all of Nice's best sights are right in the heart of the city, but it's definitely worth the shoe leather. A prime example are the dual attractions of the Parc Floral Phoenix (p111) and the Musée des Arts Asiatiques (p108). The former is home to a large population of local birdlife, as well as some 2,500 species of indigenous flora, rambling over 20 picturesque gardens. The park's programme of temporary themes and exhibitions are also well worth turning up for.

The Musée des Arts Asiatiques, on the other hand, is anything but a celebration of local culture. Devoted to Asian and Subcontinental history, this striking museum (designed by Kenzo Tange) is a refreshing stop on the culture circuit. And if earthly objects have lost their power to please, make a star trek to the Observatoire de Nice (p111), where guided tours show off the Eiffel-designed facility that surveys the city and the heavens from the summit of Mont Gros.

La Part des Anges p17

Eating & Drinking

Nice knows food. It's an immutable law that, at some point during your stay here, you will sink your teeth into something that will have you breaking out your best French in an effort to persuade the chef to part with the recipe. Which, of course, he won't. As is the case in most French towns, Nice's culinary traditions and signature dishes are as old as the city walls, and as heavily defended. Everyone has their own, jealously guarded versions of the local specialities. The most common of these are: *socca*, a delicious chickpea flour pancake, which serves as the city's principal source of fast food; *petits farcis*, stuffed vegetables with meat or herb and mushroom fillings; *pan bagnat*, which is an odd kind of compressed sandwich filled with tuna, onions, tomato, egg and olive oil; *estocafinado*, a stew of salt cod, garlic and tomato; and *tourte de blettes*, a pie filled with Swiss chard, pine nuts and raisins.

Strictly local

In the minds of many who live here, niçois cooking is synonymous with a quick, tasty meal rather than fine dining; something you might have on the way to or from a night out, or after school with the children when no one has the time or energy to cook at home. And every neighbourhood has its favourite socca stops, although Vieux Nice, it must be said, gets more than its fair share.

Distilleries Idéales p17

In the heart of the old town, Lou Pilha Leva (p61) is nothing short of a landmark. Pick up your socca, farcis, pizza, salad and the rest from the kiosk and either sit down at one of the communal tables in the street or just wander off into the crowd with your plastic glass of beer in hand. Service is fast, efficient and doesn't tolerate dithering. The same applies to Nissa Socca (p63), down by the cathedral, where aficionados say you'll find the best socca in town. Meanwhile, at Chez René Socca (p57) or the legendary Chez Pipo (p102) out by the port, even regulars expect to queue for a table.

For more substantial local grub, get yourself along to one of the city's family-run institutions, where apron and spatula have been handed from generation to generation like some kind of gastronomic relay race. Acchiardo (p54), L'Estrilha (p59), Cantine de Lulu (p75), Voyageur Nissart (p81), Lou Pistou (p61) and Restaurant du Gésu (p63) are all much-loved

examples of the genre. But perhaps the most charming of the lot is the tiny Vieux Nice shoebox that is La Merenda (p61). The absence of a phone (stop by in person to reserve) and the paucity of tables do nothing to put off the hordes of hungry punters who come by in the hope of being seated, lunch and dinner, day in, day out. Expect the ultimate version of every niçois classic from one of the most modest and talented chefs in town.

Top toques

While there's no doubt that local cuisine is king in Nice, there are still a number of restaurants that are shooting for the stars, and giving high-earning locals and blue-chip tourists something to spend their money on.

The hotel diners are topping the list these days, with two of the top fine-dining addresses in town having had recent transfusions of young blood. Jean-Denis Rieubland has replaced the legendary Bruno

Turbot at the Negresco's Chantecler (p95) and, as we go to press, early reports are sounding promising indeed. Similarly, the Palais de la Méditerranée's Padouk restaurant (p96) has seen renowned incumbent Bruno Sohn handing over the reins to his protégé, Philippe Thomas, who has already been an integral part of the kitchen operation here for some years.

Other new moves include an ambitious project at La Réserve (p103), whose beautiful waterside premises have been transformed into an ambitious catch-all project of fine-dining, bistro and bar under the auspices of stellar chef Jouni Tormanen. Otherwise, the same names are ruling the roost, with Christian Plumail (p64) and Keisuke Matsushima (p79) both still doing wonderful things at their eponymous restaurants. And if you want to get the best of the seafood, L'Âne Rouge (p101) and Grand Café de Turin (p60) are still the safest bets – although, that said, the more modest (and, therefore, more affordable) Le Bistrot du Port (p102) roasts up a mean sea bass.

It's also worth heading a few clicks out of town to the film-set perfect surroundings of Coco Beach (p113), which has grown from a beachside fish grill in the 1930s to one of the most sophisticated seafood restaurants on the Riviera, with views that will widen even the world-weariest eyes.

Cafés & bars

Most people will be able to find somewhere in Nice for a drink that matches up pretty well with their idea of the perfect local. There are sprawling pavement cafés (especially along cours Saleya and in the squares, where the extra space allows for a bit of spread), down-to-earth bars, style bars, tiny family-run cafés and chi-chi tea rooms.

SHORTLIST

Best socca
- Chez Pipo (p102)
- Chez René Socca (p57)
- Lou Pilha Leva (p61)
- Nissa Socca (p63)

Best fine dining
- Le Chantecler (p95)
- Keisuke Matsushima (p79)
- Le Padouk (p96)
- La Réserve (p103)
- L'Univers de Christian Plumail (p64)

Great terraces
- Auer Gourmet (p57)
- Bar de la Dégustation (p57)
- Beau Rivage (Plage) (p94)
- La Civette du Cours (p57)
- Le Safari (p63)

Superior seafood
- L'Âne Rouge (p101)
- Le Bistrot du Port (p102)
- Coco Beach (p113)
- Grand Café de Turin (p60)

Best for vegetarians
- Zucca Magica (p104)

Best local cuisine
- Acchiardo (p54)
- Cantine de Lulu (p75)
- L'Estrilha (p59)
- Lou Pistou (p61)
- La Merenda (p61)
- Restaurant du Gésu (p63)
- Voyageur Nissart (p81)

Wines by the glass
- Cave de la Tour (p57)
- La Part des Anges (p79)
- Vin/Vin (p81)

Great value for money
- Le 22 Septembre (p54)
- La Pizza (p80)
- Restaurant du Gésu (p63)

Tea, coffee, cakes
- Auer Gourmet (p57)
- Emilie's Cookies (p63)
- Granny's (p60)

DON'T MISS

1, rue St-François de Paule 06300 NICE

Open from 7am to 11pm 7 days a week in summer
8am to 11pm 7 days a week in winter

Tel: 04.93.62.94.32

The Best Breakfasts

Tasty Lunches

Convivial Dinners

Croquettes aux chèvre
fines herbe accompagnées
la salade garnie

Among what visitors would generally consider to be the quintessentially French cafés (that is, the very busy ones staffed by waiters who pride themselves on a certain brusqueness), La Civette du Cours (p57) and its neighbour Le Safari (p63) are the hands-down favourites. Always full, their kitchens always knocking out snacks and light bites at all times of day and night, they are fun and convenient. And they're both perfectly suited for a spot of leisurely people-watching, thanks to terraces with front-row views of the daily flower market.

For a more serious drink, however, the wine selection at Cave de la Tour (p57) takes some beating. An eccentric little wine bar (whose wall-mounted mission statement reads: 'No to alcoholism, yes to fine French wines'), La Cave is great fun and richly appointed with dozens of fine local vintages. Also with a stand-out selection is Vin/Vin (p81), tucked behind the Nice Etoile shopping centre (conveniently enough: there's nothing quite like a trip to a mall to work up a good alcoholic thirst). The wine list at La Part des Anges (p79) is similarly impressive (as is the limited but delicious selection of lunchtime *plats*). Harder stuff (notably on the killer cocktail list) can be found at the ever-popular Distilleries Idéales (p58), where great beers and classic (albeit somewhat Gothic) decor will make pub fans feel right at home.

Delicate teas, great coffee and moreish pastries are in plentiful supply the length and breadth of Nice. You're unlikely to go wrong wherever you are, although the diner-like Emilie's Cookies (p75), the charming yet stylish Granny's (p60) and the sophisticated Auer Gourmet (p57) are among the best to be found anywhere in town.

Something different

For those times when nothing but an authentically spicy curry will hit the spot, Nice has two excellent refuges from the western world. First, the unpretentious (and, let's face it, really rather unfortunately named) Delhi Belhi (p58) may not be able to offer a great deal more than the standard selection of rubies (kormas, tikkas and whatnot), but what it does, it does well. Plus, there's the unusual (for those accustomed to British curry houses, anyway) bonus of a serviceable wine list. A little more upmarket and with a more ambitious menu is Le Noori's (p79), tucked in among the New Town's swankier shopping streets. Weary shoppers, office workers and tourists sit side by side to wolf down the likes of tender lamb karai.

Virtuous eating and drinking is more prevalent than you'd think in what is ostensibly a town whose restaurants are dedicated to fine food with no real thought given to the preservation of waistlines. Organic, allergy-conscious grub is produced with some élan by New Town restaurant Bio et Clo (p74), while sea-fresh sushi can leave you feeling simultaneously full and guilt-free at My Sushi (p61) and Kamogawa (p77). To wash it all down, choose from a menu of boutique mineral waters at the Water Bar (p64) or a juice, smoothie or shake at Manao (p61). Further detox opportunities await at Nocy Bé (p63), with a list of herbal teas as long as your arm. Another tea specialist, although a little off the tourist trail, is the excellent Liber Thé (p113), which also refreshes the mind with a great little bookshop, live jazz and even the occasional theatrical performance. The perfect place in which to lose a lazy afternoon.

Alziari

WHAT'S BEST
Shopping

You don't need to max out your credit card to have a decent shopping spree in Nice. Of course, there are high-end boutiques and luxury stores, but there are all kinds of affordable treasures too. Vieux Nice is packed full of quirky shops, busy markets and excellent quality, reasonably priced clothing outlets. Like any busy tourist town, Nice has its fair share of souvenir and junk peddlers, but it also has a sophisticated, fashion-conscious citizenry. And they, just like everyone else, need to do their shopping somewhere.

The great outdoors

At the heart of any great city you will always find a thriving market, and Nice is no exception.

The historic pedestrianised walkway of cours Saleya (p48) is where local flower, fruit and veg growers, and a rich assortment of regional food merchants come to set up stall every morning of the week (except, that is, on a Monday, when it's strictly a flea market). The result is a paradise for the senses, with the air perfumed by endless tubs of freshly cut flowers, and stalls piled high with sun-kissed peaches, strings of delicately pink garlic and the vivid green of artichokes, asparagus and the rest. Even if you're not shopping for anything more than a bag of apricots, it's still perfectly possible to spend a whole morning here.

Another interesting outdoor (and indoor) market is the portside

Puces de Nices (p104), where all manner of fusty objects are sold, from attractive tat to serious antiques. But if it's the spoils of the quayside itself that interest you, then you'll need to head back into Vieux Nice, where the daily Fish Market (p67) has sea creatures great and small, caught, cleaned and iced by local hands. Again, even if you're not looking to land your supper here, it's still a great place for a poke around. The shoppers haggle and the gulls gather expectantly on the surrounding rooftops as the midday wind-down draws closer.

Palate pleasers

There is, it seems, no end to the amount of high-quality food shopping that it's possible to do in Nice. Even the local grocery stores, of which there are many in the old town, have shelves piled high with mouth-wateringly fresh pasta, spun out of the machine on a daily basis, in all shapes and sizes. But to take home a southern treat that's going to last, you'll need to head down to the cours and seek out the sunny shopfront of Alziari (p65). Here you'll find more or less every product that can possibly be manufactured from the olive, both fruit and wood. There are enormous tubs of them, black, green and a couple of hues in between, all of them fresh, juicy and shining with oil. Which leads on to the next product line: rows of lambent bottles, glowing with everything from first-press, top-flight dressing oils to the everyday cooking varieties. There are even large capacity cans of the stuff for the truly hopeless addicts.

Something a little less savoury can be found at Nice's two top *confiseries*, whose specialities of jams, candied fruits and fruit-based liqueurs and preserves allow them

SHORTLIST

Best womenswear
- Blanc du Nil (p67)
- Une Cabane sur la Plage (p67)
- Chanel (p82)
- Galeries Lafayette (p84)
- Glove Me (p68)
- Secrets Dessous (p85)
- Tyche Valerie (p104)

Best jewellery
- Bijoux Burma (p81)
- Cartier (p81)

For the larder
- Alziari (p65)
- Auer (p65)
- Confiserie Florian (p104)
- cours Saleya (p48)
- La Ferme Fromagère (p82)
- Le Local (p68)

Market shopping
- cours Saleya (p48)
- Les Puces de Nices (p104)

Best menswear
- Blanc du Nil (p67)
- Espace Harroch (p82)
- Façonnable (p82)
- Galeries Lafayette (p84)
- Timberland (p85)

For the wine cellar
- Les Caves Bianchi (p67)
- Nicolas (p84)
- La Part des Anges (p79)

Best for children
- L'Atelier des Jouets (p65)
- Enfant Ti Age (p82)
- Petit Bâteau (p85)

Best under one roof
- Le Cèdre Rouge du Prince Jardinier (p82)
- Espace Harroch (p82)
- FNAC (p82)
- Galeries Lafayette (p84)
- Nice Etoile (p84)

Best for cosmetics
- Bérénice et Eglantine (p65)

Caves Bianchi

to exhibit window displays that look as if they belong in the colour plates of a fairytale book. Auer (p65) in Vieux Nice is the prettiest of the two, with its lovingly preserved 19th-century interior, while the quayside Confiserie Florian (p104) offers a glimpse behind the scenes with guided tours of its kitchens.

All good stuff for gifts, no doubt, but if it's a picnic you're planning and you've missed the market, get over to Le Local (p68), where you'll find nothing that you won't want to snatch right off the shelf and cram into your mouth. It's a tiny shop but the shelves are piled high with Sicilian wines, antipasti in jars, or freshly made in trays, cold meats, cheeses, salads, pasta – the list goes on. Alternatively, keep it strictly dairy at La Ferme Fromagère (p82), where hundreds of French cheeses are stored in meticulously monitored conditions.

Fine wines reach from floor to ceiling at the historic Caves Bianchi (p67). The shelves groan with venerable vintages, while crates of high-quality local appellations take up much of the floor space. Staff here know their stuff and, refreshingly, use their knowledge to help you find what you're looking for rather than selling you something you're not.

Top dollar

There's no getting around the fact that the Riviera is a stylish strip, and even if Nice is content to leave the glitz and glam to Monaco and Cannes, it still knows how to scrub up for a night out on the tiles. And the principal hunting ground for designer threads, jewels and accessories are the shops on and around New Town's rue Paradis.

First among these is purveyor of elegantly preppy couture Façonnable (p82). Their womenswear and jeans outlet (one virtually next door, the other opposite) flesh out the collection, but the main focus remains the flagship store, where the outer man is nattily dressed from socks to shirt studs. Which leaves the question of footwear, duly answered by high-end leather shoe store Paraboot (p85), just a few

steps away. Alternatively, designer fashion, not to mention interior design, from a wide range of quality labels can be found all under one roof at Espace Harroch (p82). Everything from fine-quality threads to sofas and day beds, spread out over four immaculately arranged shop floors.

Nice's chi-chi ladies flex their *plastique* at Cartier (p81). But because what's underneath matters too, the saucy, stylish and seductive lingerie outlet Secrets Dessous (p85) also does a brisk trade in the kind of undergarment that is guaranteed to upgrade a standard city-break to a first-class romantic weekend.

And for junior mannequins, Petit Bâteau has a wide variety of style-conscious clothing to smarten up the sprogs (for those few golden moments before their own ice-cream and sundry foodstuff motifs have been added to the pattern).

Affordable fashion

Proof that you don't need to splurge to look good is in abundant supply in Vieux Nice. Protecting heads against the Riviera sun with hats as diverse as original panamas and Kangol caps, La Chapellerie (p67) has a huge range of headwear at affordable prices. Other extremities are catered for at Glove Me (p68), handmakers of leather gloves in dozens of funky styles and colours.

The lightweight Noa Noa womenswear at Une Cabane sur la Plage (p67) is perfect for soaring summer temperatures, as are the pure cotton dresses and blouses at Blanc du Nil (p67). Both stores manage to come in well under the price radar of the uptown boutiques without conceding any style points. A similar trick is pulled off by Bijoux Burma (p81), an elegantly upmarket jewellery shop that specialises in nothing but high-quality fakes. This is where to kit yourself out with rings, bracelets and tiaras that only an expert could tell apart from the real thing.

And for the unmotivated, the uninspired and the time-poor, everything is packaged under one roof at Galeries Lafayette (p84) department store, or try the good local version, Nice Etoile (p84).

Le Smarties p24

WHAT'S BEST
Nightlife

With half of Nice's 380,000 inhabitants clocking in at under 40 years of age, you'd think that this would be prime territory for club promoters really to shake things up a bit. So it comes as quite a surprise to many visitors that the city's clubbing culture is mainly confined to the gay community (with one or two exceptions), and that the majority of the revelry here takes place against the backdrops of local bars and restaurants. Ibiza it ain't, then, but that's not to say Nice has no pulse. There are almost as many people stumbling around Vieux Nice after midnight as you'd find on an average afternoon in most other towns of this size. And if you pick the right night, you can catch some excellent bands and DJs in many of the city's bars. It's just a question, as with everywhere else, of knowing where to go.

Late drinks

Sitting in a bar nursing a last 'last drink' is the time-honoured way to spin out a good night, and Nice has many great places in which to do just that. Late-opening bars like La Civette du Cours (p57), Les Distilleries Idéales (p58), Le Keep in Touch (p96) or Bar de la Dégustation (p57) are to be found on every other corner in the old town, but you'll need to look a bit harder to find the places that offer something more than just a terrace and a drinks list.

Le Bar des Oiseaux (p68) is a good example of just such a place. Late drinks at this old-school French bar inevitably develop into something out of the ordinary, thanks to the uproarious spirit of comedienne Noëlle Perna, who runs the place in between stage shows.

Impromptu singing, stand-up comedy and even snippets of off-the-cuff theatre, you never know what might happen. Alternatively, try your luck at the similarly silly Le Six (p69), where drinks come with a cheesy side order of telephone flirting. Interconnected handsets are dotted around the bar, allowing other punters who like the look of you to ring your bell and see if you might want to maybe, like, meet up for a drink.

For a little less conversation and a lot more action, try Wayne's (p69). He'll hook you up – if not with a suitably drunken bedfellow, then at least with lots and lots and lots of beer. Expect loud bands, girls getting their tits out on the dance floor and sweaty frat boys shouting, 'Partay!' For a less raucous version, try Ma Nolan's (p61) or Blue Whales (p69).

Clubs

Glamorous grooves, with a show-boating crowd to match, can be sought out at two main addresses in town. First, Ôdace (p87), in the heart of the New Town, emanates louche orientalism from every nook, with its slickly appointed bar, restaurant and dance floor. Things get going here after midnight, when the champagne-sipping clientele get up to dance and the DJs get into some seriously funky house and garage. On a similar trip is portside Guest (p105), where Prada-clad punters strut their stuff to an upbeat housey soundtrack.

Just across the water, on the other side of the harbour, the atmosphere couldn't be more different in Blue Moon (p104). This sweaty little stew of a club whips its post-bar punters into a carefree frenzy with a no-frills mix of pumping house and handbag anthems. Catch it on the right night, and you could find yourself in the midst of a memorable party. And the same goes for the old town's Ghost (p69), another pint-sized boîte where the wide-ranging playlist (drum 'n' bass, hip hop, house and straight-ahead house) keeps the tiny dance floor in a state of happy mayhem almost every weekend.

For something a little more sophisticated, Le Liqwid (p69) and Le Before (p85) are both good places to sip a few cocktails and get on board with the DJ's jazzy warm-up set. But, when it comes to the DJ bar, Nice's premier destination has to be Le Smarties (p87). Billing itself as an 'electro lounge', this retro-hip bar is populated by the kind of clientele who don't look out of place among the decor of funky divans and 1970s television sets. Music comes courtesy of spinners with names like Miss Van Der Rohe and International DJ Gigolo.

Of course, this being the Riviera, it would be rude not to consider at least one night of gambling and large-scale cabaret. All of this, and plenty of other suitably bling-tastic diversions, are provided by Casino Ruhl (p96). In spades.

Gay & lesbian

Some of the most full-on club nights in town are run by what are, first and foremost, gay venues. Chief among these is Le Klub (p96), where clubbers of all orientations join ranks to put their hands in the air like they just don't care. Which they don't, and why would they with household names like Jeff Mills manning the decks? Of course, Le Klub hosts a good many nights that hold less of a cross-sexual appeal – every fourth Sunday, for example, when cabaret night features entertainment from large men in short skirts.

Another big favourite among the city's gay clubbers is Blue Boy (p113), where buff lads and carefree house music provide all that's required for an unbeatable night out. Meanwhile, a bit closer to the promenade is the less cruisey and more mixed Le Flag (p87), where music is appreciated with a drink in the hand rather than a shirt tied around the head.

Le Before

THE DEPARTMENT STORE
CAPITAL OF FASHION

GALERIES
Lafayette

-10 %

NICE
CAP 3000
CANNES

From:

Code: 67 393

-10%*

To benefit from this 10%* discount, present this card and your foreign passport <u>before</u> payment at any main cash register.
This discount is not refundable once payment is made and cannot be cumulated with other discounts.

* Except on services, food & beverages, books and items marked with a red dot.
Valid until Dec. 31, 2009.

12%** TOURIST TAX REFUND

- Non European Union residents.
- 12%** tax refund on total purchases over 175 €** net (after discounts deducted) made on the same day, in the same store.
- Export limit outside the E.U.: 3 months.
- The 12% tourist tax refund can be added to the 10% discount.

** Except on services, food and subject to government regulations.

GALERIES
Lafayette

NICE MASSENA - CAP 3000 - CANNES
galerieslafayette.com

* Le grand magasin capitale de la mode -

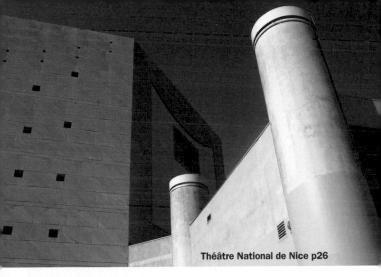

Théâtre National de Nice p26

WHAT'S BEST
Arts & Leisure

In many ways, Nice's greatest asset is its geography. With 7.5km (4.5 miles) of coastline and 300 hectares (740 acres) of parks and gardens, the city is abundantly equipped with picturesque outdoor spaces. Add to that a climate that rarely dips below 'pleasantly cool' and it's easy to see why much of life is conducted out in the open. Sport is a big deal in Nice, from in-line skating along the promenade des Anglais through to sub-aquatic explorations of the coastline. But it's not all about the body: culture vultures will find rich pickings among the theatres, opera and cinema. And if you time your visit right, you can take in world-class acts at the various music festivals that take place throughout the year, notably in July when the Nice Jazz Festival raises the curtain on some of the big names in the business.

Under the sun

The life aquatic is at the top of most sporty visitors' agendas, with a whole raft of activities in, on and under the water to choose from. Although, if you'd prefer a slightly less littoral approach, you'll also find a number of excellent indoor and outdoor sporting facilities, as well as acres of open space on which to hone those in-line skating skills.

For the tougher tourist who is not averse to a touch of healthy muscle ache, sea kayaking is one of the most memorable ways to explore the coastline around the Baie des Anges. Les Eskimos à l'Eau (p100) is the foremost organiser of kayaking jaunts both around the port in Nice and inland, along the fresh waterways of the Var and Verdon. Setting to sea in a slightly larger craft probably has a

Poseidon

wider appeal, however, and a short stroll along the quayside reveals a stack of options, from the yacht charter deals at Moorings (p105) to the simple day trips offered by Nice Diving (p105) and Poseidon (p105). The latter two outlets specialise in Nice's underwater sights, of which there are a good many. Introductory trips for snorkellers and first-time divers are especially popular in the summer season.

Back on dry land, the main pastime is in-line skating (as you'll soon notice when strolling along the promenade des Anglais on a sunny day). Get your skates on at Roller Station (p96) and Nicea Location Rent (p88), and set to it on the promenade or else in the Jardin Albert 1er. Novices welcome the safety in numbers (and the fact that the roads are closed to traffic) on the second Friday night of every month, when Nice Roller Attitude (p97) skate club has its good-humoured cruise around town.

On stage

Theatre, music and dance are all taken very seriously in Nice, where big international acts and world-renowned performing arts companies are regular billings. Aside from annual events, such as the swinging Nice Jazz Festival (p31) or the Festival de Danse (p33), most of the action takes place at a handful of key venues.

Chief among these is the Théâtre National de Nice (p88), whose programme of French and foreign classics, and commitment to nurturing upcoming talent has gained considerable acclaim. And turning a similar discernment on the worlds of opera and classical music, the Opéra de Nice (p69) pulls in performances from some of the most established companies and orchestras on the circuit, as well as new material from the bleeding edge of contemporary dance and New Music.

Nice is also a popular stop-off on the modern music scene, with the larger venues like Acropolis (p87) and Théâtre Lino Ventura (p114) pulling in all the usual big names, along with some more underground hip hop and electronic music outfits. The mega gigs tend to take place at Palais Nikaïa (p114) or at open-air venues out of town.

But it's not all international in flavour: a brace of niçois theatres, Théâtre du Pois Chiche (p69) and Théâtre Francis Gag (p69), have some of the most well-trodden stages in town. Which is quite an achievement considering almost all of their performances (from reinterpretations of Molière through to urban rap) are given in the local Niçois dialect.

On screen

The most erudite film programing to be found in town takes place at the Cinémathèque de Nice (p88), which tends to fold in a healthy dose of classics with its regular diet of quality offerings from contemporary world cinema. All films are screened in *version originale* (that is, subtitled rather than dubbed – non-French speakers should keep an eye open for movies in English).

Another decent *version originale* cinema is the Rialto (p88), where five air-conditioned theatres tend to draw passing anglophone punters on their way to and from the nearby promenade. Expect a fairly mainstream selection of movies, from blockbusters to smaller budget new releases.

Health matters

After all that sun and salt water, what the body needs is a cool, quiet retreat to restore the tissues. Enter La Bulle d'Isis (p88), Nice's premier spa and beauty salon.

DON'T MISS

SHORTLIST

Best classical and dance
- Festival de Danse (p33)
- Les Nuits Musicales de Nice (p32)
- Opéra de Nice (p69)
- Théâtre National de Nice (p88)

Mega gigs
- Acropolis (p87)
- Palais Nikaïa (p114)
- Théâtre Lino Ventura (p114)

Local theatre
- Théâtre Francis Gag (p69)
- Théâtre du Pois Chiche (p69)

Best cinemas
- Cinémathèque de Nice (p88)
- Rialto (p88)

For wellbeing
- La Bulle d'Isis (p88)
- Hi Hôtel (p136)

For the body
- Les Eskimos à l'Eau (p100)
- Moorings (p105)
- Nice Diving (p105)
- Nice Roller Attitude (p97)
- Nicea Location Rent (p88)
- Poseidon (p105)
- Roller Station (p96)

Best for live music
- Acropolis (p87)
- Le Bar des Oiseaux (p68)
- Le Blue Whales (p69)
- Ma Nolans (p61)
- Nice Jazz Festival (p31)
- Palais Nikaïa (p114)
- Théâtre Lino Ventura (p114)
- Wayne's (p69)

To go for a run or to take a walk
- Jardin Albert 1er (p94)
- Parc du Château (p54)
- Parc Floral Phoenix (p111)
- promenade des Anglais (p89)

Calendar

Carnaval de Nice p30

The following are the pick of the annual events that take place in Nice and Cannes. Further information can be found nearer the time from flyers and the seasonal guides that are produced by the respective tourist offices (p157). For gay and lesbian events, look out for *Le Klub* magazine. The dates given below are those that were announced as we went to press, but obviously arrangements do change. Thus to avoid disappointment, we recommend that you consult the relevant website or organisers in advance.

January

Ongoing Luna Park (see December)

1 New Year Concert
Acropolis, p87; Opéra de Nice, p69
www.opera-nice.org

See in the new year with music courtesy of the Philharmonique de Nice.

6 (2008) **Prom Classic**
promenade des Anglais
www.promclassic.com
This is a keenly contested and much discussed ten-kilometre (six-mile) foot race along the length of the promenade des Anglais.

12-13 (2008) **Salon du Marriage**
Acropolis, p87
www.lunedemiel.com
From flower arrangements to honeymoons, plus bridal dresses to make a princess envious displayed on the catwalk, this vast wedding show has it all.

February

13-17 (2008) **Festival International des Jeux**
Palais des Festivals et des Congrès, Cannes
www.festivaldesjeux-cannes.com
See box p34.

Nice Jazz Festival p32

16 (2008) **Carnaval de Nice**
Various locations, Nice
www.niceccarnaval.com
This famous Mardi Gras carnival sees
flower-strewn floats battling it out,
ending with the burial of the Carnival
King on the promenade des Anglais.

Mid Feb **Paris-Nice International
Cycling Race**
Punishing race whose finish line is on
the promenade des Anglais.

March

Ongoing Carnaval de Nice (see
February)

1-31 Mars aux Musées
Various venues, Nice
www.nicetourism.com
Special deals and coordinated exhibitions around the city's museums.

Early-mid Mar **Nice Côte d'Azur
Boat Show**
Port of Nice
www.nicecotedazurboatshow.com
Messing about in boats.

8-17 (2008) **Foire Internationale
de Nice**
Acropolis, p87
www.nice-acropolis.com
International trade fair.

April

1-6 (2008) **Festival C'est
Trop Court**
Cinéma Rialto, p88; Théâtre de la
Photographie et de l'Image, p71
www.nice-filmfest.com
Annual short-film festival.

Early Apr **Baie des Anges Regatta
Baie des Anges**
Promenade & Beaches
www.nicetourism.com
More messing about in boats.

Early-mid Apr **Festin des
Cougourdons**
Jardins de Cimiez, Cimiez
www.nicetourism.com
Eccentric, much-loved annual gathering to compare strangely mutated,
locally grown gourds.

20 (2008) **Nice Half Marathon**
promenade des Anglais
www.nicesemimarathon.com

Easter Sunday Easter Egg Hunt
Parc Floral Phoenix, p111
www.nicetourism.com

May

1 May Day
Various locations, Nice and
Cannes
Singing, eating, drinking and dancing
round the May Pole.

Mid May **TriMed Regattas**
Baie des Anges, Promenade &
Beaches; Port
Even more boat-related fun.

17-18 (2008) **La Nuit des
Musées**
Various venues, Nice and Cannes
www.nuitdesmusees.culture.fr
The fourth year of a Europe-wide festival that sees participating museums
opening its doors free of charge from
9pm to 1am.

29-31 (2008) **L'Italie à Table**
promenade des Anglais
Italian food growers and producers
exhibit their wares on the promenade.

Mid-late May **Festival de Cannes**
Palais des Festivals et des
Congrès, Cannes
www.palaisdesfestivals.com
The international film festival

June

Ongoing L'Italie à Table (see May)

21 (2008) **Fête de la Musique**
Various locations, Nice
www.fetedelamusique.culture.fr
Free national music festival.

Mid June **Nice en Roller**
promenade des Anglais
Two-day rollerblading meeting that
takes over the promenade with skaters
of all ages and abilities.

22 (2008) **Ironman France Nice
Triathlon**
promenade des Anglais
www.ironmanfrance.com

S H O R T L I S T

Festival de Cannes

Hippest festival haunts
- Amiral Bar (p121)
- Bar des Célébrités (p121)
- Le Loft (p127)
- Volupté (p124)

Best for star-spotting
- Le 72 Croisette (p121)
- Café Roma (p122)
- Le Palme d'Or (p123)

Best for glam get-ups
- Christian Dior (p124)
- Fendi (p124)
- Louis Vuitton (p124)

Best party spots
- Le Loft (p127)
- Morrison Lounge (p127)

**Best for sleeping among
the celebs**
- Le Carlton (p143)
- Hôtel 3.14 (p144)
- Majestic Barrière (p147)
- Le Martinez (p147)
- La Villa d'Estelle (p148)

Cheapest festival digs
- Le Festival (p144)
- Hôtel Embassy (p147)
- Hôtel Molière (p147)
- Hôtel Oxford (p147)

Best deal-making lunches
- 38 The Restaurant (p119)
- Le Mantel (p122)
- Le Palme d'Or (p123)

Best antidotes to the bling
- Forville Market (p127)
- Ile Saint Honorat (p129)
- La Taverne Lucullus (p123)

Best power breakfasts
- Cannelle (p122)
- Volupté (p124)

Trendiest terraces
- Bar des Célébrités (p121)
- Café Lenôtre (p122)

DON'T MISS

Moonlight and music

High above the city in the heart of the ancient quarter of Le Suquet, a series of concerts unfolds in the small courtyard that adjoins the Eglise Notre-Dame d'Espérance. Les Nuits Musicales du Suquet is a well-respected annual event in the classical music calendar, and yet not all of its recitals conform to the stereotype of *recherché* chamber music and esoteric choral pieces. The festival's organisers are, it seems, perfectly prepared to take risks to keep Les Nuits (which celebrates its 33rd year in 2008) as fresh and innovative as possible. And 2007 was no exception to this rule.

On the last night of the festival, a large crowd turned out to see French indie star Camille perform a rendition of Britten's *A Ceremony of Carols*. During part of the performance, entitled *Prières du Monde*, a series of a capella renditions of indigenous prayer songs from around the world saw Camille searching deep in her diaphragm for all kinds of ticks and noises. Her purpose was apparently to remind us that, different as we are, there are certain spiritual threads that bind us all together. Reactions were mixed, but whether spectators came away from this display eulogising over its integrity or lamenting its pretentiousness, the object of the evening had been achieved. No one would know quite what to expect the following year, or indeed, the year after that.

Known as the 'cradle of the European triathlon', Nice drops everything when the time comes to host this annual swim, bike and run fest.

27-29 (2008) **Festival du Livre de Nice**
Jardin Albert 1er, p94
www.nice-livre.com
Annual round of debates, talks, readings and events as authors and readers descend on the city.

29 **Fête de la Mer**
L'Eglise du Jésus, p52
Traditional fishermen's procession from the church to the beach culminating in the ceremonial burning of a boat.

Late June **Fête du Château**
parc du Château, p54
www.feteduchateau.com
Lively modern music festival featuring funk, jazz, trip hop, Latin and rock acts over two evenings (starts at 7pm).

Mid-late June **Festival de Musique Sacrée**
Various churches in Vieux Nice
www.nice.fr
Sublime choral and instrumental religious masterpieces performed by international artists.

July

14 **Bastille Day**
Various locations, Nice and Cannes
Expect fireworks on Nice's promenade des Anglais and Cannes' Croisette.

Mid-late July **Nice Jazz Festival**
Jardins de Cimiez, Cimiez
www.nicejazzfest.com
One of the biggest international jazz festivals in Europe, which is set among the picturesque gardens abutting L'Eglise et Le Monastère Notre Dame de Cimiez (p107).

Mid-late July **Festival International de l'Art Pyrotechnique**
La Croisette, Cannes
www.palaisdesfestivals.com
Spectacular fireworks contest that sees rival nations competing to win the Vestals d'Or award.

Le Village de Noël p34

Mid-late July **Les Nuits Musicales du Suquet**
L'Eglise Notre-Dame d'Espérance, Cannes
www.nuitsdusuquet-cannes.com
See box p32.

Mid-late Aug **La Castellada**
Parc du Château, p54
www.nice.fr
Series of musical concerts and period theatrical pieces set in the grounds of the ruined chateau.

Late July **Fête du Malonat**
Locations around Vieux Nice
www.nice.fr
Time-honoured celebrations in honour of the *Vierge de Malonat* (who banished the plague from what was then the *quartier* of Malonat).

August

Ongoing La Castellada (see July)

Early-mid Aug **Les Nuits Musicales de Nice**
L'Eglise et Le Monastère Notre Dame de Cimiez, p107
www.nice.fr
A large programme of chamber music concerts.

15 **Feast of the Port**
Port de Nice
Traditional quayside food festival.

Mid Aug **Pantiero**
Palais des Festivals et des Congrès, Cannes
www.festivalpantiero.com
Getting a name for itself on the international dance and rap music scenes, this festival draws big-name acts like Dilated Peoples and Cut Chemist.

Late Aug **Festival de l'Art Russe**
Palais des Festivals et des Congrès, Cannes
www.palaisdesfestivals.com
Cinema, dance, gastronomy and much more in honour of Russian culture.

September

1-30 **Septembre de la Photo**
Théâtre de la Photographie ct de l'Image, p71; Various venues, Nice
www.tpi-nice.org
Coordinated photography exhibitions.

3rd week Sept **Journées du Patrimoine**
Various locations, Nice and Cannes
www.culture.gouv.fr

A chance to poke your nose in where it doesn't belong. Historic and government buildings open their doors to the public, before slamming them again.

October

Ongoing **Septembre de la Photo** (see September)

Early Oct **Blues Festival**
Palais Nikaïa, p114
www.nikaia.fr
Get your mojo working at Nice's premier blues festival.

November

Early Nov **Festival MANCA**
Various locations, Nice
www.cirm-manca.org
Workshops, concerts and other events from budding music students.

9 **Nice-Cannes Marathon**
promenade des Angais
www.marathon06.com
The course starts at Nice and goes winding up the coast road.

Mid-late Nov **Festival de Danse**
Palais des Festivals et des Congrès, Cannes
www.festivaldedanse-cannes.com
Modern dance in all its avant-garde, cutting-edge glory.

December

Dec-early Jan **Le Village de Noël**
place Masséna, p78
www.nicetourism.com
A lively Christmas fair that includes an ice rink as well as stalls and entertainment for all the family.

Mid Dec **Baie des Anges Rowing Race**
Baie des Anges, Promenade & Beaches
www.nicetourism.com
More boats.

Late Dec-early Jan **Luna Park**
Acropolis, p87
www.azurpark.com
Indoor amusement park with the all-new Vortex ride, among many others.

Movers and shakers

Board games, dice games, card games, ball games, mind games... it's just wall-to-wall playtime at Cannes' annual Festival International des Jeux. And it really is international too, with games enthusiasts crossing continents just to dawdle among the hundreds of stalls set out in the Palais des Festivals, looking at other people's ideas of good, clean indoor fun. Most people, though, just wander in off the street to pick up a few pointers on Sudoku, bridge, Go, Scrabble – the list goes on.

Not to be outdone by its cinematic counterpart, Cannes' games festival has created its own version of the Palme d'Or. The As d'Or Jeu de l'Année (awarded each year to the best new game) has fast become the most coveted prize in gaming. Previous winners have included the hectic party game *Time's Up!* (in which players assume identities as diverse as Fred Astaire and Prometheus), while 2008's shortlist sees a board game set in Jack the Ripper's Whitechapel pitted against an power struggle centred in 16th-century Persia. And yet, as bonkers as it sounds, it's all surprisingly good fun.

The festivities in 2008 will kick off with an exhibition tracing the history of game-playing in India with displays of more than 1,500 games. And that's not all: the fifth world championship of carrom will take place at the same time. Who says the film festival gets all the glamour?

Itineraries

Nice In...

... a morning

Half a day isn't long to see a city, so the best strategy, rather than attempting a whistle-stop tour of the sights, is to go straight to the heart of the matter and confine your wanderings to the neighbourhood that best reflects the character of the place. This, of course, is **Vieux Nice**.

Start off at **cours Saleya** (p48), and get there as early as possible, so you can see the city's famous flower market in full swing. Fragrant corridors of blooms, and stall after stall of locally grown fruit and veg line this historic street. Linger long enough to buy a succulent white peach or a bunch of glistening grapes to munch on the way, then turn north at the far end of the cours, heading up rue Jules Gilly. A short way along this street, you'll come to the homely cluster of pavement tables that

announces **Granny's** café and crêperie (p60). Stop here for a quick slurp of coffee, then press on northwards, to **rue Droite**.

You have now arrived at the main artery of Vieux Nice. As you ascend this gently sloping street, you'll notice on both sides a proliferation of private galleries, exhibiting the work of the city's established and upcoming artists. Do a bit of window-shopping as you make your way to the top, where you'll find **Palais Lascaris** (p54) on the left.

Inside this historic 17th-century villa, beautiful frescoes, statues and works of art are preserved like insects in amber among the atmospheric rooms and stairways. It is free to all, and has some fascinating, quirky corners (not least the 18th-century apothecary, which is straight out of Hammer House of Horror). Once you feel ready to rejoin the modern world,

ITINERARIES

Musée National Message Biblique Marc Chagall p38

head back down rue Droite and take the first available right on to rue Rossetti. Opening out before you is Nice's prettiest square, and towering over it, the magnificent **Cathédrale de Sainte Réparate** (p49).

If time is on your side, have a look inside the cathedral, whose triptych of organs are something of a mecca for musicologists, but there's still plenty to see, so don't linger long. From place Rossetti, head south and turn right on to rue de la Préfecture, which skirts the edge of the spacious place du Palais. From here, you will be able to admire the **Palais de la Préfecture** (p54) and the **Palais de Justice** (p53), but since there's no public access to these buildings, it's best to press on towards the boulevard Jean Jaurès.

Once you reach the boulevard, turn left and stroll down towards **place Masséna** (p78), Nice's newest and most controversial public space. Pause to see the fountain (at the southern end of the square) do its thing, then follow the curve round to the tranquil **Jardin Albert 1er** (p94). This would be a good place to find some shade and rest your legs for a few moments, as you watch the dog-walkers, perambulating mums and tourists potter past. When you're done, cross the road on to the promenade des Anglais and strike out eastwards. It's time for lunch.

When you reach the gorgeous art deco sign that announces the steps leading down to **Plage Beau Rivage** (p94), you've reached your destination. In summer months, it's probably wise to make a booking at the beach's restaurant **Beau Rivage (Plage)** (p95), where you can end your tour with a good brasserie lunch, *les pieds dans l'eau*.

... a day

What a difference a day makes. Not only will you have the chance to follow the itinerary above, but you can cap it off with an afternoon of high culture. For this, you will need to head north, to **Cimiez**.

There are any number of municipal buses that will take you there, but if you want to get the real

Parc du Château

flavour of the areas that stand between you and hilltop Cimiez, wait at the designated stop for **Nice Le Grand Tour** (p94). Get a top-deck seat on this open tour bus, plug in your earphones and let yourself be led through Nice's glorious, if sometimes turbulent past. The stop you want is 'Musée Matisse', at the crest of the avenue des Arènes de Cimiez, whose broad, sophisticated streets are lined with luxurious villas dating from the Riviera's golden age of winter tourism and aristocratic pleasure-seeking.

But the pleasures are purely aesthetic at **Musée Matisse** (p108), where artfully distributed personal items combine with an exhaustive collection of the artist's paintings, drawings and cut-outs to conjure a complete picture of the man and his work. Just a few hundred yards from the imposing Regina (a former hotel, where

Matisse spent some highly productive years), the museum succeeds in conveying a real impression of intimacy, as if the artist himself had just stepped out of the room.

From here, you have two choices. Either stick around and have a wander through the past at the **Musée Archéologique de Nice-Cimiez** (p107), just next door, followed by a stroll in the gardens of the **Monastère Notre Dame de Cimiez** (p107). Or turn on your heel and walk back down the hill towards **Musée National Message Biblique Marc Chagall** (p111).

The first option will guarantee a certain sense of detached calm, either among the impressive Roman remains in the grounds of the Musée Archéologique or in the fragrant arbours and cypress-shaded walkways of the monastery's gardens. Some of the best views of the coast can be had from these gardens, which adjoin the larger public park that hosts Nice's annual jazz festival.

If, however, your cultural appetite has been whetted, take the Chagall option and immerse yourself in the vivid dreamscape of this extraordinary collection of biblically themed paintings. And once you're done, there's a superb café in the museum's grounds, just right for an afternoon pick-me-up.

Then it's back on to the Grand Tour bus (there are stops outside both the Matisse and Chagall museums) and back into town. Revisit the place du Palais for an aperitif at **Bar de la Dégustation** (p57), then wander back down towards the promenade.

It's at this time, just as the heat is starting to leave the sun and the crowds are thinning out, that many Niçois choose to have their daily swim. Join them: there is nothing quite like the cool embrace of the Med after a hard day's marching from sight to sight. Dry off on the pebbles, then slip back into your clothes and head to **Le Grand Café de Turin** (see p60) for some of the finest *fruits de mer* to be found anywhere on the coast.

... 48 hours

Day one is taken care of in the itineraries outlined above, which leaves the luxurious question of how to fill a whole other day in Nice. Well, why not start off slowly with a dose of serious relaxation at the **Hi Hôtel** (p136)?

The commitment to design at this funky urban retreat extends as far as its slickly appointed hammam, where non-guests can book in for a morning session of cleansing and purification in the artfully lit, subtly scented steam room. You'll find pots of herbal tea and thick white towels

considerately distributed around the minimalist chill-out area, inviting you to sacrifice a few hours of your life to serene oblivion. But you must resist; there is still much to see.

Get your kit back on and come floating into the street, where you'll need to head east. Cross boulevard Gambetta, passing the pretty Jardin Alsace-Lorraine on your left, and head down rue Rivoli. This will bring you out next to the historic **Hôtel Negresco** (p141), which has provided room and board for many a Woosterish wanderer and incognito crowned head in its time. Cross on to the promenade and scan the horizon for a Pinocchio ice-cream cart (they're plentiful along this stretch). It's time for a retox.

Next up, the **MAMAC (Musée d'Art Moderne et d'Art Contemporain)** (p71). Adjust your course northwards and, by the time you've finished your ice-cream, you'll have reached the forecourt of the MAMAC. Spend the run-up to lunch admiring the best of the moderns, then slip into nearby Mediterranean restaurant **Oliviera** (p63) for a serving of sunshine on a plate.

After lunch, take yourself to a higher level, via the lift at the foot of the 19th-century Tour Bellanda, which makes the 90-metre (295-foot) ascent to the **Parc du Château** (p54) so much more bearable. From the top, you will be able to see clear across the Baie des Anges and, when you finally turn your back on the magnificent view, you'll have an afternoon's worth of exploring to do among the stately gardens, monumental cemeteries and whimsical waterfalls of this delightful city park. And, come evening, drinks, dinner and dancing will be spread out before you as you emerge at the bottom of the stairs of Montée Lesage, right back in the heart of Vieux Nice.

Boulangerie J Multari

Give Us This Day...

The French are obsessed with their bread. It's a well-known national characteristic: in the same way that your average Brit is prey to an irresistible, genetically coded impulse to discuss the weather, his continental counterpart is ruled by a similar urge when it comes to the subject of baked goods. The phrase 'daily bread' still has some currency in France, where the best boulangeries turn out batch upon batch of loaves and pâtisseries to a steady stream of customers. Day in, day out. What better way, then, to get the feel of a city than to work your way from one boulangerie to the next, beginning at breakfast, breaking for lunch and rounding the day off with a teatime pastry?

This itinerary covers all three of these meal points, so you'll need to set aside the morning and the best part of the afternoon to complete the whole thing. A fair amount of eating is involved, but then there's

a fair amount of walking too, so consciences can remain clear.

Shop for breakfast at the perennially busy **Boulangerie J Multari** (p81). Look for its mint-green façade and, inevitably, a queue of shoppers stretching out into the street. Try to arrive early (they open at 6am, but any time before 10am is fine), not to beat the crowds (you should expect a small queue at any time of day) but to ensure that you get the full choice of croissants, brioches, cakes and tarts that are freshly baked here every morning. The choice, which is immaculately arranged in antique display cabinets beneath sky-blue ceiling frescoes, is large, but the patience of the busy staff is notoriously short. In other words, it's best to have an idea of what you want before you step inside.

Most of your fellow shoppers will be in here for a baguette or two, a handful of croissants – that

ITINERARIES

sort of thing. But this is a special outing, which calls for something a little more fancy than the average morning gap-filler. Why not, for example, a raspberry-filled croissant or *feuilleté*? Or the rich caramelised sugar rush of a mini *tarte aux pommes*? Fluffy wheels of *pain aux raisins* are dotted with plump currants, while beneath them, phalanxes of cream- and fruit-filled pastries join ranks with more elaborately teetering stacks of confectioner's custard and gossamer layers of choux pastry.

Resist the breads for the time being – although take note of some of the more unusual varieties, all baked on '*pierre naturelle*', as you may want to grab a loaf before shipping out to the airport. Get your breakfast bagged up, then set off in an easterly direction along rue de la Liberté. After a few minutes' walk (having crossed the broad avenue Jean Médecin with its view across the pedestrianised tundra of **place Masséna**), turn right on to rue Alberti and pull in at no.9, **Emilie's Cookies** (p75).

This is where to stock up on take-away coffee or juice (or both) – they froth up a mean latte here. Try to resist picking at your pastries as you continue down rue Alberti – the picnic spot is almost in sight.

Turn right on to avenue Félix Faure and follow the road round to **Jardin Albert 1er** (p94), where you'll find picnicking opportunities by the hamperload. Sit on a bench and watch Nice go by as you breakfast. This is the city's oldest public garden and it's where you'll get the best chance to see the real rhythm of local life. Workers use this as their short cut into town, joggers and in-line skaters zip past along the crisscrossing pathways, and you'll find relaxed old-timers doing much the same as you, taking a time out on the benches for a spot of people-watching.

Make your way out of the park in a westerly direction, which will take you past Bernard Venet's giant steel sculpture, whose shape was intended as a tribute to the azure scimitar of Nice's coastline. With this in mind, cross the street

Cours Saleya

ITINERARIES

on to the promenade, head down to the beach and have a nice, long cooling swim. You'll need to work up an appetite for lunch.

The venue for this meal is not so much a local boulangerie as a link in a chain that provides local boulangeries to cities across the world. **Au Pain Quotidien** (p57) has branches from Brussels to Manhattan, via Moscow and Dubai, but what makes the Nice version special (apart from the quality of its bread) is its peerless location, right among the market stalls of **cours Saleya** (p48). So, when you've had enough of the beach, head back across the promenade and enter Vieux Nice through one of the little arched walkways beneath the historic **Ponchettes**. These vestiges of the city's ancient past (which have been used as fish market, *lavoirs* and much else besides) now house the arty **Galerie des Ponchettes** (p91), and the artwork has even spilled outdoors in the form of a discreet mural (tucked away on your left, depicting a man on a ladder).

By the time you arrive at the cours, the market will be starting to wind down for the day. This is the moment when the last-minute bargains on just-ripe fruit and blooming flowers are to be had – have a quick look around and see what you can find. Then grab a table at Pain Quotidien before you get your feet hosed down by the street cleaners, and while there are still seats left in the bakery.

You'll find a large range of breads to choose from (wheat, rye, spelt and so on) but the most famous loaf baked here (in stone ovens) is the sourdough. Sandwich fillings are made daily and so the selection tends to vary, but it's really the bread that you're here for, so take a seat at one of the smaller tables (or, if you're feeling sociable, the long communal one) and wait for it to arrive. Meanwhile, enjoy the front-row views of the market provided by the large storefront windows on all sides.

After lunch, wend your way north through the streets of Vieux Nice until you hit rue du Collet François, which opens out on to place Saint François, with its pretty fountain (and perhaps still some evidence of morning's fish market). From here, take any of the sweet little streets running up to place Saint Augustin, were you can pause to admire the feisty spirit of **Catherine Ségurane**, whose story is told on a small plaque next to her statue. A niçoise washerwoman at the time of the Ottoman siege of the city in 1543, Ségurane saw off the would-be occupiers with her scrappy, rabble-rousing spirit, and a few judiciously placed blows from her washerwoman's paddle.

Continue down in the lee of the colline du Château, heading towards the port on rue Sincaire (romantics will appreciate the Foreign Legion recruitment office, to your left) and rue Catherine Ségurane. You may want to have a little look around some of the antique shops that line this street.

Confiserie Florian (p104) is just a short walk from here, heading north on quai Papacino. Visitors are allowed into the kitchens of this famous jam factory to watch the various preserves being made. This should put you in the mood for one last pâtisserie. Cross to the other side of the port and head north up rue Arson until you reach no.20, the final bakery of the day: Boulangerie Lagache (04 93 19 04 38).

Eat your fill and then walk it off as you head back to Vieux Nice, this time taking the coast road around the **quai Rauba Capeu**.

War Memorial p46

Make The Memories Stick

Countless artists have made a picture out of this city; indeed some of them, most famously Matisse, remained hopelessly in its thrall throughout their lives, never quite managing to gel with other surroundings. Perhaps it is, as Matisse claimed, the quality of the light here, or perhaps it's those quirky sightlines that suddenly appear in Vieux Nice's cobweb of narrow streets: the unexpected little square; a checkerboard of sun-battered shutters. Whatever the reason, one thing is beyond discussion: Nice is a pretty city. In fact, it's so photogenic that even the clumsiest clicker can, with a little

guidance, snap a masterpiece. And so, with this in mind, pick up your camera and spend a morning (when the light, they say, is at its best) on the trail of the city's perfect picture.

Photo opps abound in Vieux Nice, where you'll see any number of tourists along the cours Saleya snapping merrily away. But our starting point is somewhere a little off the beaten track, just a few minutes walk north, at the tiny place du Gesù and its Baroque masterpiece, the **Eglise du Jésus** (p52). This is your first picture.

The church is unusually narrow, and yet it looms with considerable drama over a quirky little square,

most of which is taken up with the sprawling terrace of **Restaurant du Gésu** (p63). Framing these tables in the foreground, aim high and try to catch the first winks of the morning sun on the church's ornate blue and yellow façade. From here, walk down rue du Gesù on to place Rossetti and see what you can make of the **Cathédrale de Sainte Réparate** (p49). Its size, together with the high probability of unsightly crowds, tends to stack the odds against the possibility of getting a decent photo, but have a go nonetheless. A telephoto lens might yield good results, especially when aimed high towards the intricate Genoese-style tiling on the dome.

Once you're done, cut across to rue de la Boucherie and follow the road round to the north until you get to place Saint-François. This is

where the **Fish Market** (p67) gets into full swing early every morning, and amid its bustle and noise you'll find picture-perfect tableaux of French life. Start with some close-ups of the fish and seafood that are spread out on the stalls. Some of them are artfully arranged on seaweed and beds of jewelled ice, others are strewn across bloody butcher's blocks in a gory still life of severed heads and iridescent scales. Crab claws shut tight with thick rubber bands, mackerel with dark tiger-stripe markings and snow-white scallops provide a medley of contrasting textures and colours.

Next, take a few steps back and frame up some of the transactions that are taking place. The watchful stallholders (who may, by the way, not like being photographed – always ask first), the haggling shoppers, and the bored old men, left to one side as their spouses gossip like, well, fishwives. Once you think you've got the shot, leave the old town behind you and walk out on to boulevard Jean Jaurès. En route towards the promenade, you'll come to **rue Alberti** (on your right). Turn up here, and get your camera out again.

There's a Greenwich Villagey vibe to this sweetly cosmopolitan street, with its many hip cafés and funky terraces. Snap away: perhaps a shot of the whole street, looking north, with **Le Haricot Magique** (p77) in the foreground. Stop for a coffee or a bite to eat before pressing on to boulevard Dubouchage at the top of the street. Take a left and, as the road transforms in to **boulevard Victor Hugo**, appreciate the change in architecture from the narrow, shuttered streets of Vieux Nice to these rows of grand townhouses. You may decide that some of the buildings are worth a picture (especially their ornate doors and porches), but your next designated stop is at the end of the street, on the south-west corner of **Jardin Alsace-Lorraine**. Here you'll find a wonderful octagonal clock mounted on a post. Frame it in the foreground, against the sky-blue shutters and wrought-iron balconies of the building behind it. Once the shutter's been released, head south down boulevard Gambetta.

This is the final phase of your quest for the perfect picture and, in many ways, the most picturesque stretch of the walk. As you turn on to the **promenade des Anglais** (heading east), you'll pass some of Nice's most famous landmarks. First up, on your left, is the iconic **Hôtel Negresco** (p141), whose distinctive dome and signage are to be found on postcards in every *tabac* in the city – see what you can

do to get a new angle on it. Looking upwards from near the entrance might be the best shot, although the hotel's doorman (part of whose job is to see that the entrance remains uncluttered with camera-clutching tourists) might disagree. A little further along, you'll find the imposing façade of the **Palais de la Méditerranée** (p141), along with the signs announcing the various beaches (especially **Plage Beau Rivage**; p94) will appeal to art deco fans.

As the promenade becomes the quai des Etats-Unis, follow it round on to **quai Rauba Capeu**, where the colour of the sea is an exquisite turquoise. Looking back across the Baie des Anges, you will get some good panoramic shots, but facing in the other direction (east), there is the appealing foreground of the rocks that cling to the edge of the road, with their streaks of lichen and discarded tatters of marled rope. Continue this way, walking around the headland, until you come to the **War Memorial** (p101). This, appropriately enough, is the final destination.

The drama of its imposing temple design, hewn into the rock face of the colline du Château, is a photographer's dream. But perhaps the most powerful shots are the more tightly cropped framings of the thousands of names that are carved into the walls and stairs, perfect in their symmetry and devastating in their number.

From here, you can either pack up your camera and take yourself back in to town, or else continue on your quest and explore the port. Perhaps you'll even get as far as **La Réserve** (p103) on boulevard Franck Pilatte, which is one of the most photogenic restaurants on the Riviera. And, by most a welcome coincidence, it also serves some of the tastiest food on the coast.

Nice & Cannes by Area

Cathédrale de Sainte Réparate

Vieux Nice

NICE & CANNES BY AREA

When exploring Vieux Nice it helps to remember that it was, until relatively recently, cut off from the surrounding neighbourhoods by the river Paillon. It was only in 1921, when the river was covered over and the Pont Vieux was demolished, that the city's most ancient quarter became fully accessible. And yet the spirit of the place remains very much one of feisty independence. It is, in no uncertain terms, the blood and guts of Nice.

Vieux Nice's new life has been the familiar modern parable of tourism and gentrification. Trendy second-homers (domestic and foreign), and a heavy traffic of tourists shuttling to the nearby airport, have brought in their wake slick bars, restaurants and shops, but the original residents are far from outnumbered. This is the part of town where the old ladies at the boulangerie still gossip together in Niçois, and where the local festivals and processions are taken very seriously.

Walking among the tall, pastel-coloured buildings of **rue Droite**, the street feels cool as a forest floor, while high above washing lines are threaded from balcony to balcony, and the faded blue shutters are shut tight against the battering sun. The unassuming façade of **Eglise de Jésus** or **Palais Lascaris** are gateways into forgotten worlds, while the sudden surprise of the **Cathédrale de Sainte Réparate**, opening up among the tiny streets, is one of the most beautiful sights on the Riviera. But perhaps the greatest of Vieux Nice's treasures is the **cours Saleya**, home to the flower market and many of the city's busiest bars and restaurants. If you have time to drink just one coffee, then drink it here.

Sights & museums

Cathédrale de Sainte Réparate

place Rossetti (04 93 92 01 35). **Open** 8.30am-noon, 2-6pm daily. **Admission** free. **Map** 51 D3 ➊

Dating from the 18th century, this impressive cathedral overlooking Nice's prettiest square was built in honour of the city's patron saint. The Sainte Réparate in question, a teenage girl martyred in the Holy Land in 250 AD, and then came the short way to France, being transported to Nice in a flower-filled boat towed by angels (hence the Baie des Anges). Modelled on Santa Susanna in Rome, the Baroque interior of Sainte Réparate mirrors the traditional basilican cruciform design and then complements that with various ornate touches, such as the brightly coloured Genoese-style tiling on the dome. Musicologists will find much to admire in the cathedral's three organs, especially the largest example (the one overlooking the narthex), which was lovingly restored in the 1970s by the renowned organ builder Jean-Loup Boisseau.

Chapelle de la Miséricorde

cours Saleya (no phone). **Open** varies **Admission** free. **Map** 51 D4 ➋

Considered one of the finest examples of Baroque religious architecture in France, this extraordinary church is almost too much to absorb in one visit. The building belongs to the Pénitents Noirs brotherhood, a religious fraternity established in the 14th century, but its opulent design dates from a few centuries later, during the golden age of the Baroque period (and indeed of the Pénitents Noirs themselves, before the intrusion of the French Revolution). The frescoed ceilings, and soaring blue and gold columns create a grand backdrop for more sombre treasures such as Jean Miralhet's 15th-century masterpiece *La Vierge de Miséricorde* or Louis Bréa's painting of the same title, finished three decades later in 1485.

Cours Saleya

Map p50 C4 ➌

Ranking alongside the promenade des Anglais as Nice's most emblematic street, the cours Saleya is home to the city's famous flower market. Every

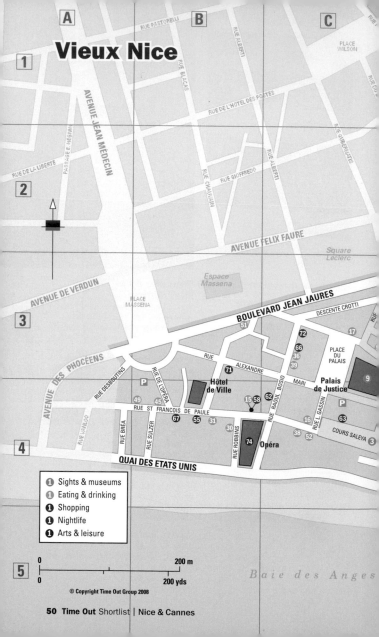

Vieux Nice

Légende:
- ● Sights & museums
- ● Eating & drinking
- ● Shopping
- ● Nightlife
- ● Arts & leisure

0   200 m
0   200 yds

© Copyright Time Out Group 2008

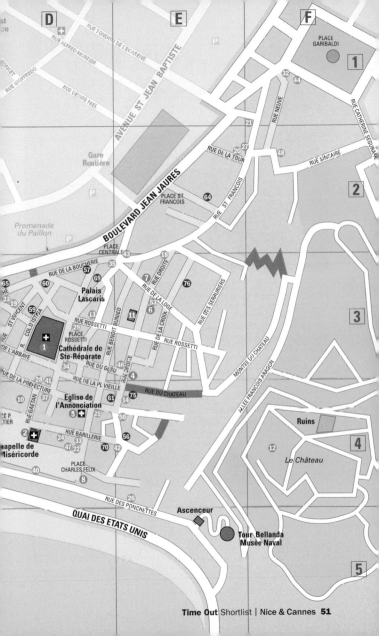

Cours Saleya p49

morning (except for Mondays, when the thrift and antiques stalls move in), this wide pedestrianised street is colonised by an army of vendors perfuming the air with endless tubs of freshly cut flowers, and mounds of deliciously ripe fruit and veg. Traders travel in from the surrounding countryside, their vans groaning with the burden of everything from strings of pinkish garlic to lush bunches of herbs and sun-kissed peaches. The market is operational from dawn (when mustardkeen locals and bleary-eyed kitchen boys are the only browsers around) to lunchtime (the ideal opportunity to pick up last-minute deals on perfectly ripe tomatoes or soft, juicy pears which are a picnicker's dream come true).

L'Eglise du Jésus

place du Gesù (04 92 00 41 90). **Open** 2.30-5pm Tue, Thur. **Admission** free. **Map** p51 E3 ❹

Officially called Saint Jacques Le Majeur, but known to everyone simply as the Eglise du Jésus, this tiny Jesuit-built church is a masterpiece of Baroque architecture and a must-see for anyone with even a passing interest in the decorative style of that period. Its narrow and towering façade was restored in the 19th century, more than 200 years after the initial construction of a church on this site, and it was during this period that the ornate blue and yellow Baroque decorations were added. Once inside, examples of symbolic Baroque artistry are evident quite literally from floor to ceiling (starting with the simple tiles beneath your feet, representing the material world of men, and ascending to the elaborately frescoed ceilings, where lambent depictions of paradise illuminate the half light).

L'Eglise de l'Annonciation

1 rue de la Poissonnerie (04 93 62 13 62). **Open** 7.30am-noon, 2.30-6.30pm daily. **Admission** free. **Map** p51 D4 ❺

Watching over the noise and commotion of the city's thriving fish market, this gilded gem of Baroque miniaturism receives a steady flow of devout locals and curious tourists through its doors. Officially, the church is devoted to Saint Jacques (or Saint Giaume, as the Niçois prefer to call him) but it is popularly associated with Sainte Rita,

L'Eglise de l'Annonciation

patron saint of hopeless causes. And it is in her name that those banks of candles flickering optimistically among the statues and pews have been lit.

Galerie du Château
14 rue Droite (04 97 13 32 17).
Open 10am-noon, 2-6pm Tue-Sat.
Admission free. **Map** p51 E3 ⑥
An exhibition platform for young local artists, this ambitious and innovative municipal gallery puts a great deal of energy into creating spicy, provocative shows. Recent exhibitors include the Monaco-based artist Elisabeth Allaria.

Galerie Jean Renoir
8 rue de la Loge (04 93 13 40 46).
Open 10am-noon, 2-6pm Tue-Sat.
Admission free. **Map** p51 E3 ⑦
Another of the city's feisty little municipal galleries (Galerie du Chateau, just around the corner, is part of the same gang), Jean Renoir is a champion of up-and-coming, young local talent. Temporary exhibitions feature a broad spectrum of work, from installations to painting and sculpture, by a variety of new artists. It's free and always worth a look – perhaps you'll be catching one of tomorrow's stars on the rise.

Matisse's House
1 place Charles Félix. **Map** p51 D4 ⑧
Demarcating the eastern end of cours Saleya, this splendid townhouse is where Matisse spent the second half of the 1920s and early '30s, conducting his life and work on the third and fourth floors. The building itself (tall, elegant, the colour of wet sand on a sunny day) shows no evidence of its famous tenant (you'll not find a museum or even a commemorative plaque) and it is not open to the public, but it is more or less unchanged since the time of the artist's stay here.

Palais de Justice
place du Palais. **Map** p50 C3/4 ⑨
One of the most impressive buildings in neo-classical style in Nice, the Palais de Justice was built in the 1880s to house the city's law courts. While visits are not offered, the façade of the building is worth taking the time to look at. Or else just sit down for a breather on the sweeping staircase that leads to the busy square (where street vendors hawk engravings, vintage posters and books ranging from pulp detective fiction to historical texts).

Palais de la Préfecture

rue de la Préfecture. **Map** p51 D4 ⑩

With its grand gates and colonnaded façade, this magnificent building looks every bit as regal as its architect had intended when it was first constructed as the 18th-century Palais Royal to accommodate the governors and princes of Savoy. Following Nice's reunification with the rest of France in 1860, the Palais became affiliated to the Préfecture des Alpes-Maritimes. It is now the seat of the region's administrative dignitaries and, as such, is not open to the public.

Palais Lascaris

15 rue Droite (04 93 62 72 40). **Open** 10am-6pm Mon, Wed-Sun. **Admission** free. **Map** p51 E3 ⑪

Construction of this magnificent if rather sombre villa was begun in 1628 by the Lascaris-Ventimiglia family, from whom it was taken during the Revolution. A century and a half of neglect saw it reach a dilapidated state until the City of Nice acquired it in the 1940s and converted it into what it is today, a historical monument. Working upwards, you'll find on the ground floor an 18th-century pharmacy, while the broad Baroque staircase leads through a series of rooms and landings decked out with frescoes, tapestries and some assorted statuary. A captivating collection of antique musical instruments on the third floor is, however, the most likely thing to detain visitors.

Parc du Château

Montée du Château/Montée Montfort (04 93 85 62 33). **Open** *Apr-May* 8am-7pm daily; *June-Aug* 8am-8pm daily; *Sept* 8am-7pm daily; *Oct-Mar* 8am-6pm daily. **Admission** free. **Map** p51 F4 ⑫

Casting its shadow over the eastern quarter of the old town, this craggy hill may no longer be the site of the chateau from which it takes its name but it does boast a well-tended park, not to mention the definitive view of Nice and the Baie des Anges. If you don't have the puff to climb the several flights of stairs that tackle the 90-metre (295-foot) ascent from Montée Lesage, there is a lift service that operates from within a grotto-like corridor next to the 19th-century Tour Bellanda (the only vestige of the former castle). The journey up costs €1.10, which is about the same as the bottle of water you'll inevitably consume if you attempt to do it on foot. At the top, you'll find breezy green spaces, a children's playground, plenty of shady nooks and an artificial waterfall. The northernmost reaches are occupied by two cemeteries, one of them reserved for the city's Jewish residents, the other the final resting place of restless Garibaldi.

Eating & drinking

Le 22 Septembre

3 rue Centrale (04 93 80 87 90/ www.le22septembre.com). **Open** 7-11pm Mon-Sat. **€**. **Budget**. **Map** p51 D3 ⑬

Simple, affordable cooking and well-sourced, equally wallet-friendly wines are the secrets to the immense success of this fun, cheap and cheerful bistro. Fans of London's Little Bay will feel right at home with the menu, whose stroganoff, pavé and sea bass all clock in at well under a tenner. Savvy students, boracic couples and budget city-breakers are all aboard the gravy train.

Acchiardo

38 rue Droite (04 93 85 51 16). **Open** noon-1.30pm, 7-10pm Mon-Fri. Closed Aug. **€€**. **Niçois**. No credit cards. **Map** p51 E4 ⑭

Mr and Mrs Acchiardo run this wonderful local restaurant with the help of their two children, much to the delight of its many regulars and those tourists lucky enough to have been pointed in the right direction. Wood panelling and gingham tablecloths make for a traditional, cosy dining room, where well-rendered versions of homegrown classics (*merda de can*, say) and the (more than) fairly priced wine list let you in on a local secret: you've stumbled across a real gem.

Au Pain Quotidien p57

Pots of gold

Auer Gourmet's rainbow of quality teas.

If you're looking for a cuppa, you've come to the right place. Newly opened and already a thriving success, **Auer Gourmet** (p57) is the small adjunct to the family's chocolate and candied fruit shop next door, which has been knocking out sweets to locals for nearly 200 years. Now, though, Auer has decided it's time for something savoury.

Functioning mainly as a tearoom, Auer Gourmet also has a wide selection of (canned and jarred) deli goods, all of them savoury, and many of them used in the small but perfectly formed lunch menu. Expect a *plat du jour* (*confit de canard*, say, or smoked salmon salad) alongside several simple dishes built around the shop's products (foie gras, *soupe de poisson* – that sort of thing). These are really little more than assembly jobs, albeit filling the midday gap with considerable style, but the main reason to come here is to sample the selection of Kusmi leaf teas.

These teas, from the luxury Paris-based importer, encompass a comprehensive range of classic brews (from English Breakfast through to Darjeeling and decaff Earl Grey), which tend to come served *nature*, maybe with a slice of lemon on the side (you'll need to ask for milk). But to find the most exciting teas on the menu, you'll need to go a little off-piste from the norm. Take the 'Spicy Chocolate', for example, which is a richly infused variety with all the depth and punch of a Viennese hot chocolate. Or, at the opposite end of the spectrum, the 'Thé Vert à la Menthe de Nanah' is a marriage of Chinese gunpowder green tea and the classic Moroccan mint infusion. The result is like a spa treatment in a cup – perfect for laying to rest a heavy lunch or chasing away the ghost of the previous evening's wine.

Sit inside, at one of the sweet little 'tea shoppe' tables or outside on the terrace, in the shade of the imposing Opéra.

Auer Gourmet

7 rue Saint François de Paule (04 93 85 59 95). **Open** 9am-1.30pm, 2.30-6pm Tue-Sat. **€€**. **Café**. Map p50 B4 ⓯
See box p56.

Au Pain Quotidien

1 rue Saint Francois de Paule (04 93 62 94 32). **Open** 7am-7pm daily. **€**. **Café**. Map p50 C4 ⓰
Another link in the popular Belgian chain, this branch of Pain Quotidien is especially suited to a lazy breakfast or brunch. High ceilings and huge storefront windows make the most of the morning sunshine, while great jams, good muesli and fine coffee fuel conversation at the long communal tables.

Bar de la Dégustation

7 rue Préfecture (04 93 80 57 57). **Open** 7am-2am daily. **€**. **Bar**. Map p50 C3 ⓱
The yellow awning and umbrellas of this popular locals' bar offer a welcome spot of shade from the sun that beats down on to the place du Palais. At least that's the excuse of the crowds of slow-sippers and sarnie-snackers who populate its terrace from morning to night.

Bar du Coin

2 rue Droite (04 93 62 32 59). **Open** noon-2pm, 7-10pm Tue-Sat. **€€**. **Pizza & pasta**. Map p51 E2/3 ⓲
Those prepared to forgive this tiny pizza joint its trompe-l'œil murals will have their tolerance rewarded with thin and crispy discs of dough topped with interesting ingredients. The 'Mme Plouck', which sports sliced potatoes, cured ham and *reblochon*, is a pizza revelation. Service is of the familial variety, and for anyone above six foot, a quaffable rosé is on hand to dull the pain of limited leg room.

Casa Mia

4 rue Pontin (04 93 85 51 72/www. casamianice.com). **Open** 7-10pm Mon, Tue, Thur-Sat; noon-2pm, 7-10pm Sun. **€€**. **Italian**. Map p51 D3 ⓳
Colourful furniture and, if anything, an even more colourful cuisine give this

central trattoria a lively, easygoing appeal. The *saveurs d'Italie* promised on the little billboard outside may take the form of aubergine bruschetta (with the aubergine taking the place of the bread) or rather more traditional meat (saltimbocca, say) and pasta dishes (from *chicche* to spaghetti).

Cave de la Tour

3 rue de la Tour (04 93 80 03 31). **Open** 7am-7pm Tue-Sat; 7am-noon Sun. **€**. **Wine bar**. Map p51 E2 ⓴
'No to alcoholism, yes to fine French wines' proclaims the sign that hangs in the bar of this superb wine shop, bar and restaurant. An interesting selection of local wines (Bellet, Lérins, Villars) complements fine niçois specialities, but this is first and foremost a well-patronised, much-loved, blokey bar.

Chez René Socca

2 rue Miralheti (04 93 92 05 73). **Open** 9am-10pm Tue-Sun. **€**. No credit cards. **Socca/pizza**. Map p51 F1 ㉑
Yes, it's cheap, but don't necessarily expect them to be cheerful at this legendary socca stop. Stern waiters slam down your drinks and you have to fetch the steaming niçois specialities yourself – but the undeniably delicious grub and the street-side views from the rustic wooden tables make it all more than worthwhile. Chez René is a local institution, as emblematic of Nice as the 'prom des ang'.

La Civette du Cours

1 cours Saleya (04 93 80 80 59). **Open** 8am-1am daily. **€**. **Bar**. Map p51 D4 ㉒
Whether outside on the sprawling terrace or inside among the mosaic tiles and huge black-and-white photos, this bar is infectiously fun and a great spot for an *apéro*. There's also a long list of bruschetta, crêpes and sandwiches if dinner still seems a long way off.

Côté Marais

4 rue Pontin (04 93 80 95 39). **Open** noon-2pm, 7-10pm Tue-Sun. **€€**. **Modern European**. Map p51 D3 ㉓

Minding their language

The conservationists of Nice's dialect.

The Niçois dialect is fighting for its life and at the forefront of this linguistic revival are two theatres operating within Vieux Nice: **Théâtre Francis Gag** (p69) and **Théâtre du Pois Chiche** (p69). The eponymous Francis Gag, a much-admired guardian angel of Nice's dialect, kept the spoken word alive through numerous plays, productions of *chants niçois* (traditional songs of the region) and hundreds of radio broadcasts spanning almost half a century. Now, though, since the death of Gag Senior, it has been left to his son (who runs the theatre) and to the city of Nice (who owns it) to continue the campaign. And they're certainly not lacking in energy. Performances range from productions of obscure Niçois plays or reinterpreted classics from the quill of Molière through to modern theatre that sees the stage occupied by everyone from rap artists to dance troupes tackling regional folkloric routines.

It's eccentric stuff, but the enthusiasm is infectious. And around the corner at the Théâtre du Pois Chiche audiences are treated to a similar range of styles, with the emphasis on the survival of the Niçois dialect. Resident writer and director Serge Dotti is a pioneer in the field, with many of his shows accessible for the Niçois novice. The marionette shows, in particular, are a great laugh.

Inside this little red box of a bistro you can choose from a wide selection of modestly ambitious dishes such as goat's cheese infused with lavender and honey served with smoked duck and baby salad leaves. Organic ingredients boost the flavour factor, and occasional chimes drifting across from the nearby cathedral keep the holiday vibe alive.

Delhi Belhi

22 rue Barillerie (04 93 92 51 87). **Open** 8pm-midnight Mon-Sat. **€€**. **Indian**. **Map** p51 D4 ㉔
Despite the unfortunate name, this tiny curry house has a menu to satisfy all but the most elaborate cravings for a good-quality ruby. Far-flung dishes you won't find, but if it's a tandoori chicken, a madras or a korma you're after, then look no further. There's also a serviceable wine list, just to remind you that you're still in France.

Les Distilleries Idéales

40 rue de la Préfecture (04 93 62 10 66). **Open** 9am-midnight daily. **€**. **Pub**. **Map** p51 D4 ㉕
Discerning punters come to this quirky corner bar to do their drinking and carousing, due in no small measure to the louche, slightly Gothic decor (exposed brick bar, stained glass window, spooky lanterns). Other attractions include suppable beers (Murphy's, Pelforth, Edelweiss), a nightly happy hour and killer cocktails.

Don Camillo Créations

5 rue des Ponchettes (04 93 85 67 95). **Open** 7-10pm Mon; noon-2pm, 7-10pm Tue-Sat. **€€€**. **Haute cuisine**. **Map** p51 E4 ㉖
In the lee of the Colline du Château, Don Camillo's low-key façade (it would be easy not to notice on this otherwise residential street) belies its interior of white linen tablecloths and accomplished modern cuisine. Expect inventive and playful dishes, such as pan-fried foie gras served with a millefeuille of *pissaladière* and socca, baby leaves and anchovy vinaigrette. Not the priciest restaurant in town, but not cheap.

Lou Pilha Leva p61

L'Escalinada

*22 rue Pairolière (04 93 62 11 71/
www.escalinada.fr)*. **Open** noon-2.30pm,
7.30-10.30pm daily. €€. **Niçois**. No
credit cards. **Map** p51 E/F2 ㉗
Half a century on, and this charming
bastion of niçois cooking is going
strong. A small cluster of tables spills
down the steps from the terrace, while
diners inside are treated to the equally
picture-postcard view of lumbering
wooden beams and a cute little spiral
staircase. All in all, a pretty restaurant,
albeit unpretentiously so, serving time-
worn local classics like the house specialities of *panaché de beignets*, stuffed
courgettes and tripe *à la niçoise*.

L'Estrilha

*11-13 ruelle de l'Abbaye (04 93 62 62
00)*. **Open** 7-11pm Mon-Sat. €€.
Niçois. **Map** p51 D3/4 ㉘
It's a good thing that this old-school
family restaurant is only open for dinner. For one thing, you need a full day's
exercise to work up the appetite to
tackle the house speciality, an earthen-
ware 'amphore' brimful of hearty fish
stew. And secondly, having acquired a
taste for said 'amphore', there's a
chance you wouldn't bother to eat anywhere else. Which would be a shame.

Fenocchio

*2 place Rossetti (04 93 80 72 52/
www.fenocchio.fr)*. **Open** 10am-
midnight daily. €. **Ice-cream**.
Map p51 D3 ㉙
Thinking outside the (ice) box, this
famous *glacier* has created around 90
different flavours of ice-cream and sorbet. The choice ranges from the unas-
sailable high ground of chocolate,
strawberry and the rest, through a mid
dle territory of temptingly unorthodox
numbers (chestnut, say, or bergamot),
all the way to a hinterland of dairy
insanity, where things like 'chewing-
gum' are viable flavours. It's all great
fun, and finger-lickingly good quality.
Our recommendation: a Nutella and
panettone double scoop.

Le Frog

3 rue Milton Robbins (04 93 85 85 65).
Open 7pm-midnight Mon-Sat. €€.
American. **Map** p50 B4 ㉚
As a restaurant idea, you might be for-
given for thinking that Le Frog just
wouldn't have legs. But nothing could
be further from the truth. American
cooking, it seems, is in high demand,
and this busy Tex Mex bistro is the
proof. Amounting to more than just a
hill of beans, the cooking covers all the

Oliviera p63

diner classics, from T bone to down-home. And come 9pm, there's live music to help the evening along,

Le Grand Balcon
10 rue Saint François de Paule (04 93 62 60 74). **Open** noon-2pm, 7-10pm Mon-Fri; 7-10pm Sat, Sun. **€€-€€€.** **International.** Map p50 B4 ㉛
Looking a lot like a library in a stately home, Le Grand Balcon is something of a novelty in this otherwise more casual part of town. The menu, which is divided into Acts I and II (the Opéra is right next door, you see), offers suitably theatrical combinations of seafood partnered with tropical flavours like kumquat, rum and the like. There are some meat dishes, too, but *poisson* is the real passion here.

Le Grand Café de Turin
2 place Garibaldi (04 93 62 29 52/ www.cafedeturin.com). **Open** 8am-11pm daily. **€€.** **Seafood.** Map p51 F1 ㉜
In the colonnaded tunnel provided by the eaves that skirt this side of the place Garibaldi, 'Le Turin' is the best

place to come for sparklingly fresh seafood in Nice. Locals sit in classic Walrus and Carpenter pose at almost every table: replete, unbuttoned and surrounded by a debris of *fruits de mer.* Service can be testy, but the atmosphere is the real thing.

Granny's
5 place de l'ancien Senat (no phone). **Open** 8.30am-7pm daily. **€.** **Crêperie.** Map p51 D4 ㉝
Managing to be both stylish and charming (the interior looks like something out of a Cath Kidston catalogue), Granny's is the perfect pit stop for a quick crêpe and a cuppa. Great pancakes (sweet and savoury), toasties, salads, and plentiful teas and coffees draw hungry shoppers and trail-weary tourists like bees to a honeypot.

Johnny's Wine Bar
1 rue Rossetti (04 93 80 65 97). **Open** 4pm-12.30am daily. **€€.** **Wine bar.** Map p51 D3 ㉞
If you've come to France to practise your French, maybe give Johnny's a miss, since this is where the city's

anglophone population often seems to congregate for a drink and a chat. Otherwise, enjoy the friendly atmosphere, the jugs of quaffable Algerian plonk and occasional live music.

Lou Pilha Leva

10 rue Collet (04 93 13 99 08). **Open** 10am-10pm daily. **€**. No credit cards. **Pizza/socca**. Map p51 D3 ㉟

Sitting down, standing up, wandering off into the crowd – there's a bit of everything going on at this swarming hive of a socca spot. No more than a glorified kiosk with a few communal picnic tables, Lou Pilha Leva does a roaring trade in takeaway socca, pizza, *petits farcis*, salad, beer, plonk... you name it, and they'll slap it on a paper plate for you and take your money.

Lou Pistou

4 rue Raoul Bosio (04 93 62 21 82). **Open** noon-2pm, 7-10pm Mon-Fri. **€€**. **Niçois**. Map p50 C3 ㊱

From the charming lilt of its name to the sweet lace curtains and the chalkboard notice announcing the *'chaudron du jour'* that hang in its windows, Lou Pistou is every inch the loveable neighbourhood bistro. On the menu, local highlights (*farcis niçois*, *tripes à la niçoise*) rub shoulders with interesting imports (*lonzo corse*, for instance).

Manao

14 rue de la Préfecture (04 89 22 66 02). **Open** 10.30am-7pm daily. **€**. **Café**. Map p51 D4 ㊲

Calling itself an *'agitateur de saveurs'*, this tiny juice bar is fun, funky and, above all, healthy. Choose from pure juices, smoothies (with soya milk, if you'd prefer) or chance your arm on a special – possibly the 'Sésame', which scatterguns your palate with apple, dates, tahini, cinnamon and honey.

Ma Nolans

2 rue Saint François de Paule (04 93 80 23 87/www.ma-nolans.com). **Open** 11am-2am daily. **€**. **Pub**. Map p50 C4 ㊳

English is spoken, the tabloids are on the tables, pints are drunk, fry ups are

Restaurant du Gésu p63

wolfed down, big-screen sport and live bands compete for your attention: in short, Ma Nolan's is an 'oirish' pub on foreign soil. But it's a cut above the other imitation boozers, so the bottom line is, if you must do it, you may as well do it here.

La Merenda

4 rue Raoul Bosio (no phone). **Open** noon-2pm, 7-10pm Mon-Fri. **€€**. **Niçois**. No credit cards. Map p50 C3 ㊴

Not much bigger than a shoebox, always packed and delightfully informal, La Merenda serves the ultimate version of every niçois classic. To reserve, stop by in person on the day of your visit.

My Sushi

18 cours Saleya (04 93 62 16 32/www.mysushi.com). **Open** 11.30am-2.30pm, 6.30-11pm daily. **€€**. **Japanese**. Map p51 D4 ㊵

If the *plateaux de fruits de mer* at the seafood restaurants that line this part of the cours Saleya look to be too much like hard work, then get your fish

MA NOLANS
IRISH PUB

Ma Nolan's Irish Pubs:
Vieux Nice: 2 Rue François de Paule. 06300 Nice
Nice Port: 5 Quai des Deux Emmanuel. 06300 Nice
Tel: (33) 04 93 80 23 87 Fax: (33) 04 93 81 46 90
Email: info@ma-nolans.com • Web: www.ma-nolans.com

 My Sushi

Nice
18, Cours Saleya
04 93 62 16 32

Monte Carlo
2, Rue des Orangers
97 70 67 67

butchered, rolled and wrapped at this swish, clean and efficient sushi joint. There are good-value bento boxes on offer at lunchtime.

Nissa Socca

7 rue Sainte Réparte (04 93 80 18 35). **Open** noon-2pm, 7-10.30pm Tue, Wed, Fri-Sun; 7-10.30pm Thur. **€.** **Pizza/socca.** Map p51 D3/4 ④
Socca, pasta, pizza (some say the best to be found anywhere in town) and plenty more vie for your attention on the menu of this lively corner restaurant. The whole vibe is casual and friendly, highlighted by the café furniture, sunny wall paintings and flags from the local footie team. The cheap pichets of wine and beers on tap make it easy for everyone join in the general mood of bonhomie.

Nocy Bé

6 rue Jules Gilly (04 93 85 52 25). **Open** 7pm-midnight daily. **€. Café.** No credit cards. Map p51 E4 ④
The perfect watering-hole for those who don't want a hangover in the morning, this exotic *bar à thé* has a list of infusions as long as your arm. There are cushions to sit on, pastries to munch on and decadent Moroccan furnishings to make you feel like you're a million miles away, or at least on the other side of the Mediterranean.

Oliviera

8 bis rue du Collet (04 93 13 06 45). **Open** noon-2pm, 7-10pm Tue-Sat; noon-2pm Sun. **€€-€€€.** **Mediterranean.** Map p51 E2/3 ④
The tiled floor, wooden beams and white walls recreate the feel of a breezy provençal kitchen at this much-loved local restaurant. From the boxes of knobbly tomatoes that are handed out by the exuberant owner to the sophisticated cuisine, a strong commitment to top-quality regional produce is apparent in every aspect of a meal at Oliviera. Gleaming vats of locally produced olive oil are lined up at the rear of the dining room as a reminder to customers that the route from *terre* to *table* has been deliciously direct.

Pâtisserie Cappa

7 place Garibaldi (04 93 62 30 83). **Open** 8am-6pm Tue-Sun. **€€.** No credit cards. **Pâtisserie.** Map p51 F1 ④
Get under the arches and out of the sun to sample some of Pâtisserie Cappa's heavenly pastries. In summer, a small selection of exceptional own-made ice-creams and sorbets is also well worth settling down for.

La Petite Maison

11 rue Saint François de Paule (04 93 92 59 59/www.lapetitemaison-nice.com). **Open** noon-2.30pm, 7-10.30pm Mon-Sat. **€€€.** **Haute cuisine.** Map p50 B4 ④
Ladies who lunch come to La Petite Maison to do just that, rubbing shoulders with an assortment of colourful locals. But come nightfall, La Petite Maison caters to an altogether more glamorous crowd. Models, movie stars and more ordinary wealthy folk come here for such gourmet indulgences as *langouste royale*, foie gras-stuffed chicken and truffle risotto. Fine wines and discreet service complete the epicurean picture.

Restaurant du Gésu

1 place du Gésu (04 93 62 26 46). **Open** noon-2pm, 7.30-10.30pm Mon-Sat. **€€.** No credit cards. **Niçois.** Map p51 E3 ④
Locals and tourists sit side by side – always a good sign – on the pretty terrace of this unpretentious, perennially busy restaurant. Simple, delicious niçois cuisine is whisked from kitchen to table by busy, bantering waiters.

Le Safari

1 cours Saleya (04 93 80 18 44). **Open** noon-3pm, 7-11pm daily. **€.** **Bar.** Map p51 D4 ④
'Continual service throughout the afternoon' advertises the sign on the terrace at this justifiably popular brasserie. Located right in the heart of Vieux Nice, Safari stocks some decent beers, wines by the glass and gap-fillers of the tartare, *tripes niçoises* and risotto varieties. A good place to fill up.

La Table Alziari
4 rue François Zanin (04 93 80 34 03). **Open** noon-2pm, 7-10pm Tue-Sat. **€€. French**. **Map** p51 F2 ㊽
The best of the restaurants that line this steep, typically niçois little street, La Table Alziari has a charming terrace and an equally unpretentious dining room. Having taken your seat, expect to see sun-drenched regional dishes (*aubergine provençales, morue à la niçoise*) on the blackboard menu.

Terres de Truffes
11 rue Saint François de Paule (04 93 62 07 68). **Open** noon-2.30pm, 7-10.30pm Mon-Sat. **€€€. Haute cuisine**. **Map** p50 B4 ㊾
Nobody knows how many truffles they have seen and cooked over the years at this fungally themed restaurant. The kitchen turns out elegant variations on the mycological theme, such as roasted sea bass served with fennel fried in truffle butter, but they are also happy to treat more lowly dishes (the baked potato, say), to a good truffling. Nothing, it seems, is exempt from the treatment. Meanwhile, in the wood-panelled dining room, an enormous, brain-like exhibition truffle surveys the contented diners from its perch.

La Trappa
2 rue Jules Gilly (04 93 80 33 69/www.latrappa.com). **Open** 5pm-2.30am Tue-Sat. **€€. Spanish**. **Map** p51 E4 ㊿
In typical Spanish style, La Trappa opens late and dishes up good-quality tapas to a hungry crowd on their way to a night out in Vieux Nice, then a few hours later, it gets them on the rebound. And there they stay until way past bedtime, drinking, flirting and making lots and lots of noise. DJs crank out decent funk and rare groove sets, with the occasional weekend foray into soulful house.

L'Univers de Christian Plumail
54 boulevard Jean Jaurès (04 93 62 32 22). **Open** noon-2.30pm, 7-10.30pm Tue-Fri; 7-10.30pm Mon. **€€€. Haute cuisine**. **Map** p50 B3 (51)
Still going strong at this smart but unpretentious address, renowned niçois chef Christian Plumail serves up good-quality food at affordable prices. Pan-fried turbot in a hazelnut crust served with celery and basil gnocchi might be followed by poached nectarine with a soft meringue and raspberry sorbet. Add to that a cracking wine list and fine coffee, and you'll find yourself wishing you owned some trousers with an elasticated waistband.

La Voglia
2 rue Saint François de Paule (04 93 80 99 16/www.lavoglia.com). **Open** noon-2.30pm, 7-11pm daily. **€€. Pizza & pasta**. **Map** p50 C4 (52)
The splendidly futuristic pizza oven at this busy, modern Italian resembles some kind of industrial chimney. Which is oddly appropriate, given the relentless turnover of punters, both outside on the terrace overlooking cours Saleya and inside, among the plushly upholstered banquettes and exposed brick walls. Nice pizzas, decent pasta and an appetising salad bar are what they're here for.

Le Water Bar
10 rue de la Loge (04 93 62 56 50). **Open** noon-midnight Tue-Sun. **€€. Bar**. **Map** p51 E3 (53)
Well, it is everywhere and there's undoubtedly more than a drop of it to drink at this gimmicky (but refreshing) take on Vieux Nice's boozy bar scene. Bottled *eau* from around the world is the poison of choice and it comes in all forms, flavours and fizzes. But if after a couple of glasses you find thing's are getting a bit too virtuous, you'll be pleased to hear that a decent list of New World wines is also available to help you along with your retox.

L'Ybane
9 rue Préfecture (04 93 92 92 32/www.lybane.com). **Open** noon-2pm, 7-10pm Mon-Sat; 7-10pm Sun. **€€. Middle Eastern**. **Map** p50 C3 (54)
Smart, sophisticated L'Ybane does a great line in meze, offering classics like tabouleh, houmous and falafel along

with more interesting culinary snap-shots, such as *foules mesdames* or *makanek* (Lebanese sausage). And a good range of palate-pleasing cocktails means that the menu-browsing can be as fun as the dinner itself.

Shopping

Some of Nice's best local artists sell their work in the small galleries on **rue Droite**, many of them little bigger than holes in the wall. Among the most interesting are Atelier Mozaïka (no.12), Moz'art (no.33), Asselot (no.5), Dury (no.31) and Leclaire (no.29).

Alziari

14 rue Saint François de Paule (04 93 13 44 97/www.alziari.com.fr). **Open** 8.30am-12.30pm, 2.15-7pm Tue-Sat. **Map** p50 B4 ⑤⑤
Green fragrant olive oil in attractively shaped bottles (or large-capacity cans, for the hopeless addicts) and tubs of fresh, succulent olives are the main attractions at this lip-smacking bou-tique next to the Opéra. A restored 19th-century mill is used to grind the olives, and all gradations of oil are sold, from the bog standard to the seriously special. Soaps and wooden tableware are also manufactured and sold by the Alziari workforce.

L'Atelier des Jouets

1 place de l'Ancien Senat (04 93 13 09 60). **Open** 10.30am-7pm Mon, Tue, Thur-Sat; 2-7pm Wed; 10.30am-6.30pm Sun. **Map** p51 E4 ⑤⑥
Resembling one of those Hollywood depictions of an elf's workshop, this charming toyshop stocks every kind of junior gift. Puzzles, trinkets and trucks, in fact, all that you might need to stuff a stocking properly can be found on these bright and cheerful shelves.

Au Brin de Soleil

1 rue de la Boucherie (04 93 62 89 00). **Open** 9.30am-7pm daily. **Map** p51 D3 ⑤⑦
If you want to return home with a touch of provençal style to lighten your

Au Brin de Soleil

own interior decor, look no further than this treasure trove of southern French furnishings. You'll find everything to pretend you're spending *A Year in Provence* from *faïence* and bedspreads to soap and candles under this one roof.

Auer

7 rue Saint François de Paule (04 93 85 77 98/www.maison-auer.com). **Open** 9am-1.30pm, 2.30-6pm Tue-Sat. **Map** p50 B4 ⑤⑧
For several generations, the same fam-ily has been making a good living here selling all manner of *fruits confits* and sinful chocolate concoctions. The 19th-century interior has been lovingly pre-served, as have the traditions and recipes that result in the candied fruits, jams, syrups and confections lining the shelves and counters. Next door, is the savoury counterpoint with its own *salon de thé* (see box p56).

Bérénice et Eglantine

9 Bis rue Colonna d'Istria (04 93 79 69 12/www.berenice-eglantine.com). **Open** 10am-1pm, 3-7pm Tue-Sat. **Map** p51 D3 ⑤⑨
See box p86.

Fingers of fun

Vieux Nice's new *gantier* extraordinaire.

In a climate like Nice's, it might seem a foolhardy endeavour to open a shop that specialises in gloves. After all, cold hands are something of a rarity in these parts. But the owners of **Glove Me** (p68) knew what they were doing. These are no woolly mittens, but sleekly stitched, beautifully crafted fashion items, designed and produced by one of the funkiest new retailers in town.

Leather is the material of choice but, for a master glover, this is only a starting point. The first skill is to find the right kind of leather, a variety that is both supple and strong, which will adapt to the movements of the hand without losing its shape. After much experimentation at the factory (based in Italy), Glove Me settled on a few key varieties. Among them, the expensive and rare 'pekari' leather from South America, which is manufactured from young wild boars, and the aristocratic buckskin. However, more humble materials, such

as sheepskin, are also used to considerable effect.

Prices are, of course, commensurate with the level of couture, but these are artisanal products and, properly cared for, should last a lifetime. A choice of more than 40 colours in some models, and a variety of linings including silk and cashmere, bring the service as near to bespoke as it can be.

Belts, pashminas and handbags are also scattered around the shelves, all of them finished to the same exacting standards. Prices are surprisingly affordable (handbags range from €120 to €200) for what are, beyond question, luxury accessories. The gloves, in particular, are seductive, almost fetishistic items – the kind of handwear that would look at home in a Helmut Newton photo shoot. And yet, with a second branch now open in Strasbourg, it seems that Glove Me has tapped into a healthy market. Sexy hands are, it seems, a growth industry.

Blanc du Nil

11 Place du Marché (no phone). **Open**
Apr-Oct 10am-5pm daily. Closed Nov-
Mar. **Map** p51 D3 60

Only open during the warmer months,
this tiny boutique specialises in clothes
made from pure cotton. Rows of
undyed white cotton garments (from
men's shirts, trousers and shorts to
women's just about everything) hang
on an assortment of rails and bronzed
mannequins. Designs are classic, with
a touch of effortless elegance.

Une Cabane sur la Plage

37 rue Droite (04 93 76 82 46). **Open**
12.30-7pm Mon; 11am-7pm Wed-Sat;
11am-2pm Sun. **Map** p51 D4 61

Having decamped from its original
location on place du Jésus, this stylish
boutique now mainly stocks women's
clothes by Danish fashion label Noa
Noa. Feminine threads from the Italian
label, Lino Factory, also hang on the
rails, as well as the Noa Noa line of children's clothes. Styles range from
romantic, floaty cotton clothes to something quite dressy.

Caves Bianchi

7 Raoul Bosio (04 93 85 65 79).
Open 9.30am-7.30pm Mon-Sat.
Map p50 C4 62

If you want the finest wines available
to humanity and you want them now,
this might be a good place to start looking. Vintages great and small are to be
found on the shelves and in the open
crates of this delightful, historic niçois
wine shop. Regional labels are plentiful and can be quite obscure, but if you
need advice, don't be afraid to ask.
Service here is that rare combination of
knowledgeable and good-humoured.

La Chapellerie

36 cours Saleya (04 93 62 52 54/
www.chapellerie.com). **Open** 9.30am-
1pm, 2-6.30pm daily. **Map** p50 C4 63

Sun too hot? Then cover your head in
style at this well-stocked hat shop.
Caps of all colours, traditional sun hats,
demure straw hats, funky Kangol head
gear and traditionally made, top-notch
panamas line the walls and fill the
showcases. There are two other
branches in Nice, as well as one in
Marseille and a fifth in Nantes.

Fish Market

place Saint-François (no phone). **Open**
6am-1pm Tue-Sun. **Map** p51 E2 64

Comprising a few rows of trestle tables
set out around the square's central
fountain, this busy, noisy fish market
is best visited early on in the day, when

Glove Me

Opéra de Nice

the catch is fresh in from the trawlers. Then, you'll find a glistening tableau of sea life spread out over jewel-like beds of ice. Come later and the ice has melted, all but a few morsels have been sold and the gulls are gathering on the surrounding rooftops.

Glove Me

5 rue du Marché (04 93 79 75 63/ www.gloveme.org). **Open** 10am-5pm Tue-Sat. **Map** p51 D3 65
See box p66.

Le Local

4 rue Raoul Bosio (no phone). **Open** 10am-5pm Tue-Sat. **Map** p50 C3 66
Stock up for a gourmet picnic at this pretty little Italian deli. The welcoming owner has filled every square inch of his tiny premises with delectable products direct from the old country. You'll find red wine from Sicily, olive oil from all over, antipasti in jars, or freshly made in trays, alongside cold meats, cheeses, salads and pasta. And if you can't be bothered to make your own picnic, then you can ask *signor* to make you a delicious sandwich and a killer cup of coffee instead.

Molinard

20 rue Saint François de Paule (04 93 62 90 50/www.molinard.com). **Open** 10am-1pm, 2-6pm Mon-Sat. **Map** p50 B4 67
The famous perfumer from nearby Grasse keeps the citizens of Nice smelling nice through this fragrant and attractive boutique. All kinds of bottled scents are sold alongside a rainbow of soaps, oils, and scented candles.

Nightlife

Le Bar des Oiseaux

5 rue Saint Vincent (04 93 80 27 33). **Open** 8pm-12.30am Tue-Sun. **Map** p51 D3 68
Imagine *Cheers* crossed with *La Cage aux Folles*. No, that's not quite right. *Moulin Rouge* meets *Phoenix Nights*? That's not it either. The only thing one can say for certain about this unique neighbourhood bar is that it is imbued with the uproarious spirit of its larger than life proprietor, comedienne Noëlle Perna. Live bands, impromptu comedy and snippets of theatre all contribute to the mayhem. Sit back, get the drinks in and wait to see what happens next.

Le Blue Whales

1 rue Mascoïnat (04 93 62 90 94).
Open 5.30pm-4.30am daily.
Map p51 D3 ⑥⑨
A DJ or live band are usually in situ at this above-average take on 'le pub'. Decibel levels tend to proscribe any meaningful conversation, encouraging instead a fair amount of drinking, pool-playing and dancing. Which is exactly what the up-for-it crowd here is after.

Ghost

3 rue Barillerie (04 93 92 93 37).
Open 8pm-2.30am daily.
Map p51 D4 ⑦⓪
There's a speakeasy vibe at this small, progressive club (you'll even need to ring the bell to get in), where a broad playlist, ranging from drum 'n' bass and trip hop to straight-ahead house, keeps the tiny dance floor good and sweaty. It's positively hopping at weekends, with cocktail-fuelled party people getting up close and personal in the heady half-light.

Le Liqwid

11 rue Alexandre Mari (04 93 76 14 28/www.liqwid-lounge.com). **Open** 6pm-12.30am daily. **Map** p50 B3 ⑦①
Somewhere to come for a few drinks and a bit of a boogie, Liqwid is a smart, cavernous club with a menu that runs to contemporary stomach liners like tuna tartare or Thai-style prawn salad. House music, electronic lounge music and the occasional departure into French pop are what you'll find in their DJs' record bags. Dress smart.

Le Six

6 rue Raoul Bosio (04 93 62 66 64/www.le6.fr). **Open** 10pm-3.30am Tue-Sun. **Map** p50 C3 ⑦②
It's either your idea of a great laugh or a toe-curling cringe-athon, but whichever way you slice it, Le Six is unlikely to leave you bored. Punters are encouraged to communicate with each other by phone (interconnected handsets are strategically dotted around the bar), so if the one next to you rings, the idea is that you pick it up and conduct a good-natured, flirty

conversation with whoever's on the other end. But for those who would prefer to keep their dignity more or less intact, there's always a programme of above-average live music to enjoy, plus an ornate 18th-century ceiling to stare at while studiously ignoring the phone.

Wayne's

15 rue de la Préfecture (04 93 13 46 99/www.waynes.fr). **Open** noon-1am daily. **Map** p50 C3 ⑦③
Wayne's is where you'll find the touring frat boys and attendant party chicks whose loud and abrasive beach conversation might have been annoying you earlier in the day. It's only worth a visit if you're up for a night of raucous (live) music and copious boozing. The website has a gallery of girls who've had their tits out in the bar, which pretty much sums things up.

Arts & Leisure

Opéra de Nice

9 rue Saint François de Paule (04 92 17 40 00). **Open** *Box office* 9am-6pm Mon-Sat. **Map** p50 B4 ⑦④
Right on the demarcation line that separates Vieux Nice from the bustling promenade, this 19th-century opera house is a joy to behold. Red velvet and gilt furnishings, crystal chandeliers and a sophisticated, well-dressed crowd create a rarefied atmosphere during evening performances. First-rate visiting international artists come to perform ballets and symphonies, as well as opera. And as with everything, the bigger the name, the further in advance you'll need to book.

Théâtre du Pois Chiche

2 rue du Château (06 13 05 29 69).
Open according to programme.
Admission varies. **Map** p51 E4 ⑦⑤
See box p58.

Théâtre Francis Gag

4 rue Saint Joseph (04 92 00 78 50/www.theatre-francis-gag.org). **Open** according to programme. **Admission** varies. **Map** p51 E3 ⑦⑥
See box p58.

Galeries Lafayette p84

New Town

Major reconstruction work has converted the central **place Masséna** into a vast open precinct at the hub of the New Town. From here, streets branch off in all directions, offering myriad shopping and dining possibilities. Not least of which are the city's two major department stores (**Galeries Lafayette** and **Nice Etoile**), under whose collective roofs you'll be able to lay your hands on everything from socks to contact lenses. But for more exclusive addresses, head down to the blue-chip **rue Paradis**, which is, as its name implies, a kind of heaven on earth for design junkies.

But God is not only in the retail: the New Town has rich pickings for culture vultures, particularly those with a taste for the contemporary. The **MAMAC** (Musée d'Art Moderne et d'Art Contemporain)

and the **Théâtre de la Photographie et de l'Image** both contain enough material to keep even the keenest museum hound going for a couple of afternoons. And for those with junior members in tow, the fustier but no less fascinating **Muséum d'Histoire Naturelle** is stuffed to the rafters with creepy crawlies.

And unlike Vieux Nice, where the buildings are jammed tightly together, the New Town has some splendid boulevards (notably Victor Hugo), where the townhouses are grand and the restaurants correspondingly smart. But if it's just a quick bite you're looking for, the area's busiest shopping streets (France and Buffa) are just a few steps to the south, where snackeries and kiosks are wedged in among a rainbow of shops, bars, clubs and cafés.

Sights & museums

Bibliothèque Louis Nucéra
2 place Yves Klein (04 97 13 48 00).
Open 10am-7pm Tue, Wed; 2-7pm
Thur, Fri; 10am-6pm Sat. **Admission**
free. **Map** p73 F2 ❶
One of the city's most visually striking
landmarks, this library is located under
Sacha Sosno's giant sculpture *La Tête
Carée*, literally 'the square head' (right
next door to the MAMAC). Occupying
10,000sq m (108,000sq ft) of space on a
single floor, the interior is decorated in
a rich palette of red and ochre. You'd
need a membership card to borrow
books or access the library's multimedia facilities, but it's worth wandering
in for a look, if only to get a closer look
at one of Nice's most iconic buildings.

MAMAC (Musée d'Art Moderne et d'Art Contemporain)
promenade des Arts (04 93 62 61 62/
www.mamac-nice.org). **Open** 10am-
6pm Tue-Sun. **Admission** €4.
Map p73 F2 ❷
Right in the heart of the city, this
sprawling temple of white marble
enshrines a bold and stimulating collection of European and American modern
art (notably New Realism and Pop Art),
with a significant showing from the
Nice School (Arman, César, Klein and
Sosno). Sculptures and a vast mural by
minimalist artist Sol LeWitt jazz up the
museum's exterior, while the permanent
collections (featuring such artists as
Robert Rauschenberg and Niki de Saint
Phalle) are supplemented by a thought-
ful programme of temporary exhibitions (the recent Pistoletto retrospective
being a prime example).

Muséum d'Histoire Naturelle
*60 bis boulevard Risso (04 97 13 46
80/www.mhnnice.org).* **Open** 10am-
6pm Tue-Sun. **Admission** free.
Map p73 F2 ❸
If it creeps, crawls or slithers you'll find
it dried out and on display in the anti-
quated wooden cabinets of this, Nice's

oldest museum. And while junior visitors are delighting at the cephalopods
and other monsters from the deep, a
wide variety of permanent and temporary exhibitions are on hand to ensure
that everyone else is similarly trans-
fixed. The most recent addition to the
permanent collection is 'Bleu Outremer',
a mesmerising catalogue of Indian
Ocean marine life, while temporary
shows like 'Trésors de Nacre' (an investigation of the use of seashells from tools
and currency through to religious trinkets) vividly bring to life even the most
obscure subjects. Well worth a visit.

Théâtre de la Photographie et de l'Image
*27 boulevard Dubouchage (04 97 13
42 20/www.tpi-nice.org).* **Open** 10am-
6pm Tue-Sun. **Admission** free.
Map p73 D2 ❹
Life through a lens is displayed in all its
forms at this slickly appointed photography gallery. Journalism, fashion, art
and experimental photography all get
their share of wall space, digital screen
space and, in the case of the salon
Gérardpierre (which features some
splendid, grotesquely enlarged portrai-
ture), head space. The gloriously ornate
architraves and mouldings contrast
with the otherwise spartan white decor
and the clean, utilitarian presentation of
the pictures. Temporary exhibitions are
usually well chosen, always showcas-
ing new talent in interesting groupings
(as, for example, the recent 'Enfants de
Cartier' exhibition of contemporary
Canadian photography, including
works by the Sanchez brothers). Most
famous of all, though, is the annual
'Septembre de la Photo' exhibition,
which usually runs right through to
November and spills over into some of
the city's other museums and galleries.

Eating & drinking

Le 26 Victor Hugo
*26 boulevard Victor Hugo (04 93 82
48 63).* **Open** noon-2pm, 7-10pm
Mon-Sat. **€€. French. Map** p72 B3 ❺

New Town

A **B** **C**

1

RUE TRACHEL

BOULEVARD

AUTOROUTE URBAINE SUD

ℹ️

🅿️ Gare SNCF
Nice-Ville

RAIMBALDI

RUE DE L

RUE MIRON

RUE ASSALIT

BOULEVARD

RUE LAMARTINE

RUE PERTINAX

AVENUE JEAN MÉDECIN

RUE DE PA

RUE HAN

2

BOULEVARD GAMBETTA

AVENUE THIERS

AVENUE THIERS

63

36

AVENUE G CLEMENCEAU

RUE AM. DE GRASSE

RUE LOUISE ACKERMAN

RUE GUIGLIA

RUE GOUNOD

RUE AUBER

RUE PAGANINI

AVE DURANTE

RUE D ITALIE

RUE DE LA RUSSIE

RUE D ANGLETERRE

AVENUE G CLEMENCEAU

57

RUE PAUL K ARR

RUE A KARR

DÉROULÈDE

17

46

AVE MAL CHAL M

34

RUE

50

49

3

RUE BERLIOZ

RUE VERDI

RUE VERDI

RUE ROSSINI

5

RUE PAUL K ARR

35

25

47

BOULEVARD VICTOR HUGO

RUE MACCARANI

RUE EUGÈNE EMMANUEL

56

22

38

AVENUE LONGCHAMP

AVENUE

51

54

4

BOULEVARD GAMBETTA

12

RUE DE CRONSTADT

RUE DU MAL JOFFRE

55

33

21

RUE DE LA BUFFA

RUE DALPOZZO

RUE DU CONGR S

23

61

RUE DE FRANCE

27

29

30

14

RUE MASSENA

60

18

AVENUE DE SUEDE

RUE PARADIS

52

44

43

41

37

RUE DE VERDUN

Jardin
Albert 1e

Musée
Masséna

🅿️

🅿️

ℹ️

PROMENADE DES ANGLAIS

Hôtel Negresco

PROMENADE DES ANGLAIS

5

0 ——————— 300 m
0 ——————— 300 yds

© Copyright Time Out Group 2008

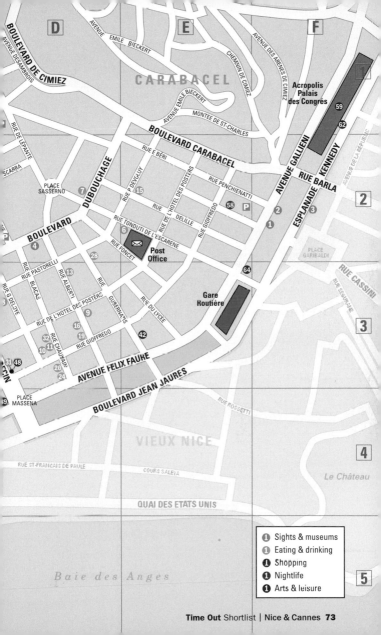

Caffé Bianco

Chef Stephane Viano caters to the well-to-do residents of this smart boulevard with a seasonal carte and an appetising daily menu of simple, hearty fare. It's an unlikely venue in some ways (from the outside, it looks like someone's house extension) but the views of the little park opposite more than compensate for the lack of architectural flair.

Amada

17 rue Tonduti de L'escarène (04 93 62 00 81). **Open** 7-10pm Mon, Sat; noon-2pm, 7-10pm Tue-Fri. **€€**. **Italian**. Map p73 E2 **6**

You could easily miss the tiny shopfront façade of this Japanese restaurant, and what a pity that would be. Deliciously light tempura, udon noodles and the rest share menu space with more inventive crossover dishes, such as the chef's takes on the niçois speciality of *petits farci* or that great bistro staple, panna cotta (made here with soya milk and a nip of ginger).

Aphrodite

10 boulevard Dubouchage (04 93 85 63 53/www.restaurant-aphrodite.com). **Open** noon-1.45pm, 7.30-9.30pm Tue-Sat. **€€€**. **Haute cuisine**. Map p73 D2 **7**

High-backed chairs, starched table-cloths and plenty of light make David Faure's upmarket restaurant a relaxed yet relatively formal address. The elegant carte (divided between *mer* and *terre*) features such enticingly simple dishes as roasted lobster tail with thyme alongside more elaborate offerings like saddle of rabbit stuffed with basil and confit shallots. Great wine list too.

La Baie d'Amalfi

9 rue Gustave Deloye (04 93 80 01 21). **Open** noon-2pm, 7-11pm daily. **€€**. **Italian**. Map p73 D3 **8**

A confirmed favourite among local pizza and pasta enthusiasts, this bustling old-style mansion has plenty to offer besides the usual. Cutlets, steaks and gambas cooked in the wood-fired oven are among the more unusual dishes, while solid favourites like saltimbocca ensure that traditionalists won't be disappointed.

Bio et Cie

12 rue Alberti (04 93 01 94 70/ www.bio-et-cie.com). **Open** noon-2.30pm Mon-Fri; noon-2.30pm, 7.30-10pm Sat. **€€**. **Organic**. Map p73 D3 **9**

See box p86.

Brasserie Flo

2-4 rue Sacha Guitry (04 93 13 38 38/ www.flonice.com). **Open** noon-2.30pm, 7pm-midnight daily. **€€**. **Brasserie**. Map p73 D3 ❿

The Flo chain has installed itself in yet another pretty shell, this time on Nice's rue Sacha Guitry, where much of the building's former incarnation as a theatre is still evident in the opulent, high-ceilinged dining room. The kitchen is where the stage used to be, the best seats are still up in the balcony. Provençal with a twist sums up the simple yet refined menu.

Caffé Bianco

9 rue Chauvain (04 93 13 45 12). **Open** noon-2pm, 7-10pm Tue-Fri; 7-10pm Sat, Sun. **€€**. **Modern European**. Map p73 D3 ⓫

A classy but unpretentious neighbourhood restaurant, Caffé Bianco is just the place to bring a new flame (or to rekindle an old one). Elegantly low-key furnishings complement an elliptical but tasteful menu that ranges from salade niçoise (from the chef's grandmother's recipe, so he says) to lamb brochettes or tuna ceviche. French wines are on hand to ply your date with.

La Cantine Bio d'Alain Alexanian

Hi Hôtel, 3 avenue des Fleurs (04 97 07 26 26/www.hi-hotel.net). **Open** 6.30am-midnight daily. **€€**. **Organic**. Map p72 A4 ⓬

See box p86.

La Cantine de Lulu

26 rue Alberti (04 93 62 15 33). **Open** noon-2pm, 7-10pm Mon-Fri. **€€**. **Niçois**. Map p73 D3 ⓭

A stronghold of regional cooking, Lulu is a fine choice for those who want to sample good-quality versions of the oft-touted salade niçoise, *merda de can* and the rest. But there's also plenty to interest the aficionado, with dishes like an authentic *daube niçoise* on the main menu and daily suggestions from the market up on the board. More elaborate dishes are cooked on a monthly basis (salt cod aioli on the first Friday, say).

La Cigale

7 avenue de Suède (04 93 88 60 20). **Open** 10am midnight daily. **€€**. **Middle Eastern**. Map p72 C4 ⓮

Smart and sleek (as you'd expect, given its location on designer-boutique row), the Cigale offers a welcome waft of spicy flavour around these parts. Lebanese is the name of the game, with sun-soaked feasts for diners (from kebabs to sticky cakes) and take-away treats for casual shoppers in the restaurant's appetising deli section.

Da Giuseppina

25 rue Delille (04 93 85 21 66). **Open** noon-3pm, 7-10.30pm Mon-Sat. Closed Aug. **€€**. **Italian**. Map p73 E2 ⓯

Worth knowing about if you find yourself caught short in this otherwise (gastronomically speaking) barren part of town, Da Giuseppina specialises in southern Italian cuisine, chiefly dishes from the chef's native Bari. Expect lots of seafood on the mouthwatering menu (combinations are often simple but rely on the outstandingly fresh quality of the ingredients – the spaghetti with clams being a memorable example). Wines are mostly Italian.

Emilie's Cookies

9 rue Alberti (04 93 13 89 58/ www.emiliescookies.com). **Open** 8am-6.30pm Mon-Fri; 9am-6.30pm Sat. **€**. No credit cards. **Café**. Map p73 D3 ⓰

There's a (Greenwich) villagey vibe to this excellent coffee shop, where the cookies in question are given the lead role in a cast of similar snacks (muffins, cakes, bagels, salads). Very tasty they are too, as are the coffees, juices and smoothies. Ideal for breakfast or lunch on the hop.

FNAC Café

44-46 avenue Jean Médecin (08 25 02 00 20/www.fnac.com). **Open** 10am-7.30pm Mon-Sat. **€**. **Café**. Map p72 C2 ⓱

The unusually high level of quality and attention to detail sets this store café apart from the rest. Even if you're not shopping there, it's worth popping in

to this bright and breezy café for a salad or a sandwich. Or even just a muffin and a decent cup of coffee.

Gelateria Pinocchio

30 rue Masséna (06 24 35 09 64). **Open** 10am-6pm Mon-Sat. €. **Café**. No credit cards. **Map** p72 C4 ⑱

An ideal bargaining chip when negotiating with weary, fractious children, this bright and twinkly little café specialises in ice-cream. There's a tantalising chiller cabinet of fruity and chocolatey flavours positioned enticingly at the entrance, as well as a few tables on the pedestrianised rue Masséna, should you want to eke out your *glace* with a coffee or a freshly squeezed juice.

Le Haricot Magique

7 rue Alberti (04 93 80 61 39). **Open** noon-2.30pm Mon-Fri, Sun; noon-2.30pm, 7.30-10pm Sat. €€. **Modern European**. **Map** p73 D3 ⑲

This groovy restaurant suits quaint little rue Alberti very well. It's a colourful, fun place with a resolutely urban clientele installed on its rustic Van Gogh style chairs. The salad bar is piled high with glisteningly fresh produce, while the menu punts an appetising combination of salads, tarts and snacks, plus a heartier dish of the day.

Indyana

11 rue Gustave Deloye (04 93 80 67 69). **Open** 7pm-midnight Mon, Sat; noon-2pm, 7pm-midnight Tue-Fri. €€€. **French**. **Map** p73 D3 ⑳

Popular with fashionistas, arty locals and stiff business suits, this smart, modern restaurant serves up contemporary French cuisine at expense account prices. Dishes range from the traditional (shoulder of lamb stuffed with girolles) to the quietly adventurous (scallop tartare with lime juice).

Kamogawa

18 rue de la Buffa (04 93 88 75 88). **Open** noon-2.30pm, 7-10pm Tue-Sat; 7-10pm Sun. €€. **Japanese**. **Map** p72 B4 ㉑

The sushi bar at Kamogawa provides time-poor tourists and office workers with sashimi, sushi and tempura, and plenty of Asahi to wash it down. But if you can spare the time, a more thorough investigation of this charming little Japanese restaurant's menu (especially the sukiyaki) won't disappoint.

Karr

10 rue Alphonse Karr (04 93 82 18 31). **Open** noon-2pm, 7-10pm daily. €€. **Brasserie**. **Map** p72 C3 ㉒

Located on a leafy stretch of the rue Alphonse Karr, this quiet and laid-back

Lina's p79

A pedestrian project?

The divisive place Masséna.

There was much ceremony when, after three long years of work, the brand-new square, place Masséna was unveiled in June 2007. Finally, the transformation was complete: what had been a sprawling roundabout choked with traffic and clogged with bus stops and taxi ranks, was now transformed into a wide-open pedestrian square. A traffic-free lung for the city, designed to filter fresh air into the heart of the shopping district and chase away the cars from the gates of the old town. And yet, when local newspaper *Nice Matin* canvassed the views of its readers, it seemed that appreciation for the new square was far from widespread.

'Worse than the Gobi desert' was one particularly blunt assessment. And indeed, talking to people in Nice, it soon becomes apparent that this is by no means an isolated criticism. The absence of any real shade is a sticking point with many locals, who tend to favour the cool and secluded walkways of nearby Jardin Albert

1er. Why, asked *Nice Matin*'s respondents, are there not more trees? Something more substantial than a handful of saplings. After all, what use is shade in ten years' time? Also sorely lamented in the survey was the absence of any flowers, or anything to add colour or character to the space.

But through the fresh eyes of a visitor to the city, many of these objections appear to be only vaguely connected to the reality of the place. A certain amount of temperature-taking was, in the end, inevitable for a population whose patience had been taxed by the long wait for this much-touted municipal asset. In truth, the square is a pleasant vista of open space after the crowded, labyrinthine streets of Vieux Nice. More than that, it is the connective tissue between the old and new quarters. There was once a river here, the now interred Paillon, so perhaps what one resident described to us as a 'sea of concrete' is an apt substitute.

bar/restaurant rustles up good risotto, as well as the usual range of bistro grub. The *plat du jour* is affordable for those looking for a place to sit, eat and sip before getting back on the move.

Keisuke Matsushima

22ter rue de France (04 93 82 26 06/www.keisukematsushima.com). **Open** 7.30-10pm Mon; noon-2pm, 7.30-10pm Tue-Fri; 7.30-10pm Sat. **€€€**. **Haute cuisine**. Map p72 B4 ㉓

One of the most respected and innovative chefs in town, the eponymous Kei Matsushima is going from strength to strength following the reopening of his restaurant in 2007. A well-deserved Michelin star now guides gastronomes, expense-accounters and well-heeled tourists to his minimalist modern dining room, where the cooking is every bit as discreetly contemporary as the surroundings. Breton crayfish, for instance, might come pan-seared with courgette-flower tempura and a lemon, saffron and fennel coulis. There's also a splendidly calming private dining room, sporting an artfully arranged cluster of wooden cooking utensils and artwork that would be just as at home in a trendy urban spa.

Lina's

14 avenue Félix Faure (04 93 85 69 60). **Open** 9am-5pm Mon-Sat. **€**. **Sandwich bar**. No credit cards. Map p73 D3 ㉔

Advertising itself as a '*créateur de sandwiches*', this square-side sarnie shop may be taking itself a tad too seriously. That said, though, it's true that they know how to slap a couple of bits of bread together, more often than not with a seriously tasty wedge of filling in between. Funky furniture and big storefront windows provide a light and cheerful environment in which to enjoy your creation.

Luc Salsedo

14 rue Maccarani (04 93 82 24 12/ www.restaurant-salsedo.com). **Open** noon-2pm, 7-10pm Mon, Tue, Fri-Sun; 7-10pm Thur, Sat. **€€€**. **Haute cuisine**. Map p72 C3 ㉕

Elegant wicker chairs and crisp white tablecloths lend just the right note of formality to this friendly neighbourhood bistro. Operating from a genteel enclave opposite the charming Église Reformée de Nice, the eponymous Salsedo changes his menu every ten days, resulting in an accomplished seasonal cuisine that draws a full house most nights. When on offer, his version of the niçois speciality *pain bagnat* is an absolute must.

Le Luna Rossa

3 rue Chauvain (04 93 85 55 66). **Open** noon-2pm, 7-10pm Mon-Fri; 7-10pm Sat. **€€**. **Italian**. Map p73 D3 ㉖

Clean, modern decor and a brief but appetising menu make this trattoria a good bet for a quick, one-course supper or an affordable, uncomplicated meal out. Choose between pasta greatest hits (penne all'arabiata, linguine with clams), a scattering of salads and assorted extras in the bresaola and carpaccio mould.

Noori's

1 place Grimaldi (04 93 82 28 33). **Open** noon-2.30pm, 7-10pm daily. **€€**. **Indian**. Map p72 C4 ㉗

A neat package of unobtrusively stylish decor and appetising subcontinental cuisine, Noori's provides the well-to-do residents of this part of town with their quota of spiciness. Just the place, then, when nothing but a lamb karni is going to hit the spot.

La Part des Anges

19 rue des Gubernatis (04 93 62 69 80). **Open** noon-2pm Mon-Thur, Sun; noon-2pm, 8-10pm Fri, Sat. **€€**. **Wine bar**. Map p73 D2 ㉘

Half wine shop, half restaurant, La Part des Anges has a delightfully endearing dual personality. A vast array of enticing bottles, from local vineyards and beyond, line the walls, while a number of small bistro tables at the back of the shop accommodate a lunchtime crowd. Expect fancy cold cuts and the odd hot dish, with more adventurous fare on Friday and Saturday nights. Wines, needless to say, kick ass.

La Pizza

34 rue Masséna (04 93 87 70 29).
Open 11am-1am daily. €€. **Pizza
& pasta**. Map p72 C4 ㉙
Perennially busy, La Pizza copes with
the demand for its services with an
increasing number of branches (notably
Le Quebec). And the reason for this
effortless popularity? Excellent wood-
fired pizzas from the gorgeous red-brick
oven, easygoing staff and democratic
pricing. A gratifyingly straightforward
and stress-free experience.

Le Quebec

43 rue Masséna (04 93 87 84 21).
Open 11am-1am daily. €€. **Pizza
& pasta**. Map p72 C4 ㉚
No, it's not a French-Canadian restaurant. This catch-all brasserie (affiliated
to La Pizza a short step down the road)
dabbles in pizza, pasta, steak dinners
and omelettes – and there's even a list
of '*spécialités américaines*'.

La Table d'Hédiard

*Galeries Lafayette, 6 avenue Jean
Médecin (04 93 62 24 92).* **Open**
9am-7.30pm Mon-Sat. €€. **Global**.
Map p73 D3 ㉛
Affordable and extremely convenient
if you're too immersed in shopping to
be scouting for restaurants, this top-
floor restaurant is a cut above most in-
store efforts. The *plat du jour* is a good
bet – something simple and fresh, anything from tartiflette to tagine – while
the menu offers a decent choice of trad
French with a token showing from the
rest of Europe and beyond. A few
local(ish) wines and smiley service also
help to restore one's energy before
another round of credit card bashing.

Tat-O-Titon

9 rue Chauvain (04 93 92 58 17).
Open noon-2pm, 7-10pm Tue-Sat;
7-10pm Sun. €€. **Crêperie**.
Map p73 D3 ㉜
Ankle-biters love it here, which means
that anyone with an aversion to children should probably steer clear of this
fun, child-friendly crêperie. The pancakes (sweet and savoury), salads and
Nutella milkshakes (yes, there is more
than one kind) are all good. Laptop tot-
ers should also note that Tat-O-Titon
has Wi-Fi connectivity.

Il Vinaino

33 rue de la Buffa (04 93 87 94 25).
Open 7-11pm Mon; noon-2.30pm,
7-11pm Tue-Sat. €€. **Italian**.
Map p72 B4 ㉝

Bijoux Burma

The excellent, freshly made pasta and a quaffable piedmontese house wine are just two reasons to come to this friendly, good-value little restaurant. Portions are hearty, and trattoria classics like osso bucco are turned out to a high standard.

Vin/Vin

18 rue Biscarra (04 93 92 93 20).
Open noon-2.30pm, 7-10.30pm Mon-Sat. **€€**. **Brasserie**. Map p72 C2 ❸

Looking very smart after its new orange and grey paint job, this popular wine bar and restaurant is continuing to attract hungry shoppers, office lunchers and a post-work crowd with its casual formula of decent food and fine wines. About a dozen wines are available by the glass (they change pretty regularly), or there's a wider choice by the bottle. Food is a combination of laid-back brasserie classics (tartare, tuna steak and whatnot) with a support act of seasonal dishes and off-the-cuff dailies (Spanish lomo, a succulent cut of cured pork tenderloin, when we last stopped by). Friendly service and a sunny terrace too.

Les Viviers

22 rue Alphonse Karr (04 93 16 00 48). **Open** noon-2pm, 7-10pm Mon-Sat. **€€€**. **Fish**. Map p72 C3 ❸

A bicameral affair (bistro on one side, fine dining on the other), Les Viviers is one of the premier addresses in town for top-notch seafood. On the extensive menu, traditional dishes of bouillabaisse and pan-fried turbot sit alongside more exciting combinations (red mullet stuffed with mozzarella and served with fusilli and cherry tomatoes, for example). A suitably grand wine list provides further refreshment.

Voyageur Nissart

19 rue d'Alsace Lorraine (04 93 82 19 60/www.voyageur-nissart.com). **Open** noon-2pm, 7-10pm Tue-Sun. **€€**. **Niçois**. Map p72 B1/2 ❸

Celebrating its centenary in 2008, this much-loved family restaurant can truly claim to have handed down its recipes through the generations. And they've accumulated quite a few of them, as evidenced by the ever-changing menu (devised each day after the morning's perusal of the market). Despite its exposed granite and wooden beams, the dining room is not so much fusty and traditional as breezily provençal. Staff are always happy to explain the menu (indeed, are used to doing so, given the relatively high number of non-locals most mealtimes).

Shopping

Avenue Jean Médecin is well stocked with branches of national and international outlets, such as **FNAC**, Zara (no.10), Virgin Megastore (no.15) and Footlocker (no.31). And on a more exclusive note, rue Paradis has a number of high-end boutiques, including **Façonnable**, **Chanel**, Kenzo (no.10), Sonia Rykiel (no.3) and Emporio Armani (no.1).

Bijoux Burma

16 avenue de Verdun (04 93 87 95 88). **Open** 10am-7pm Mon-Sat. Map p72 C4 ❸

What a fantastic idea: a slick, classy jewellery shop, which at first glance appears to be stuffed full of diamonds, but is in fact selling affordable, good quality fakes. Kit yourself out with rings, bracelets and tiaras that only an expert could tell apart from the real thing. Cartier is just doors away, too, if you want to compare.

Boulangerie J Multari

2 rue Alphonse Karr (04 93 80 00 31). **Open** 6am-8.30pm Mon-Sat. Map p72 C3 ❸
See p40.

Cartier

4 avenue de Verdun (04 92 14 48 20). **Open** 10am-12.30pm, 2-6.30pm Tue-Sat; 2-6.30pm Sun. Map p73 D4 ❸

Perhaps you've heard of it? You know, dealers in exquisite jewellery, high-end timepieces and leather goods. Yes, that Cartier. This link in the golden chain of boutiques is just the same as its counterparts in terms of the assurance of quality, service and (let's face it) stratospheric prices that its name implies. Still, if you have the cash to splash, this is undoubtedly one of the chicest places to find out what you'd look like encrusted in diamonds.

Le Cèdre Rouge du Prince Jardinier

6 avenue de Verdun (04 93 16 83 10/ www.princejardinier.com). **Open** 10.30am-1pm, 2-7pm Tue-Sat. **Map** p72/73 C/D4 **40**

Only a handful of these beautiful shops are to be found scattered around France, so lucky Nice for having one right on its doorstep. Always chic, never showy, the range of garden furniture, crockery, lighting, glassware and elegant gardening paraphernalia is to die for.

Chanel

6 avenue Paradis (04 93 88 39 99). **Open** 10am-7pm Mon-Sat. **Map** p72 C4 **41**

From the minimalist symmetry of its façade to its tidily chic interior, even the shop itself is like some kind of elegant packaging. Still, what else would you expect from one of the high-rollers of ladies' fashion? Seriously expensive, achingly stylish outfits (with bags and shoes to match) are there for all to see and the select few to buy.

Enfant Ti Age

3 rue Gubernatis (08 73 65 89 79/ www.enfant-ti-age.com). **Open** 10am-12.30pm, 2-7pm Tue-Fri; 10am-7pm Sat. **Map** p73 E3 **42**

Brainchild of a local designer, this children's furniture, toy and textile store has the unusual pedigree of a stock that combines aesthetics with an element of sturdiness that will be reassuring to most parents of young children. Beds, chests, chairs, seats, lighting, curtains – there's pretty much everything you'll need for kitting out one good-looking nursery. It's not cheap, and some of the toys are possibly a little too whimsical to get any real play time, but it's certainly worth having a look.

Espace Harroch

7 rue Paradis (04 93 82 50 23). **Open** 10am-12.30pm, 2-6.30pm Tue-Sat. **Map** p72 C4 **43**

Three floors of style, either in the form of designer togs or interior design, is what's on offer at this sleek boutique. Clothing ranges from top-notch labels like Helmut Lang, Paul Smith and Yamomoto cater to men and women, while everything from furniture to tableware and incense is available in the home furnishings department. Below decks, there's a basement café serving lunch and drinks to weary shoppers.

Façonnable

7 rue Paradis (04 93 16 22 35). **Open** 10am-7pm Mon-Sat. **Map** p72 C4 **44**

The menswear label that began with this shop now has stores in every major city, selling elegantly preppy sportswear, suits and formalwear. A few doors up and across from here, Façonnable womenswear and Façonnable Jeans also punt their own variations on the theme. Prices are what you'd expect from a chic Riviera fashion store.

La Ferme Fromagère

27 rue Lépante (04 93 62 52 34). **Open** 8.30am-1pm, 4.30-7.30pm Tue-Sat. **Map** p72 C1 **45**

The main reason to come to La Ferme is to browse its wonderfully pungent cheese shop, which sells literally hundreds of meticulously cared for French cheeses. Almost every region of the country is represented, with a good range of cheese-friendly wines to boot. The adjoining fromage-themed restaurant is fun for a fondue.

FNAC

44-46 avenue Jean Médecin (08 25 02 00 20/www.fnac.com). **Open** 10am-7.30pm Mon-Sat. **Map** p72 C2 **46**

A branch of the national multimedia megastore, this FNAC is a fine example of what is so great about these slick and sophisticated outlets. At heart, it's a bookstore, with a floor or two set aside for books (fiction, biography, magazines, travel guides, newspapers,

Creative platforms

The fine art of tram construction.

Leading up to its inauguration in November 2007, Nice's tramway was gradually transformed into a network of high-profile works of art. The idea, to commission 15 artists to supply pieces of work for certain key stops, has produced some striking results. This is our pick of the best.

Place Masséna takes in the seven mounted figures of Spanish artist Jaume Plensa's *Conversation à Nice*. Intended to represent the ethnic diversity of the town, the illuminated sculptures sit atop giant poles, facing each other and passing commuters. Further up the line at square Doyen Jean Lépine is Frenchman Jean-Michel Othoniel's architectural installation *Le Confident*. The work is a large mesh of aluminium and coloured glass intertwined around two strategically placed seats.

Parisian Yann Kersalé has made innovative use of the Riviera's trademark azure by installing a series of crisscrossing neon lights above the track on avenue de Jean Médecin. The effect is particularly striking given that it is only visible at night, when much of the city's natural colour has drained away.

Exploring a medium other than the visual, French artist Michel Redolfi has created a bespoke set of jingles for each station, adapting the mood of the music and the tone of the announcements to suit each individual space. Different soundscapes have been conceived for use during day and night.

Corsican artist Ange Leccia also wanted to align his work to the changing moods of the tramway. His solution: *Disque Solaire* at Las Planas station. As its name suggests, the work is a disc that reacts to the effects of the sun. During the day, this 'boule gazeuse' absorbs solar energy, which it stores until, come sunset, the installation begins to glow, constantly fluctuating in its colour. The chromatic range of the *Disque Solaire* is as unpredictable as the weather of any given day, and will produce suitably diverse results.

Le Cèdre Rouge du Prince Jardinier p82

graphic novels), but there's also a decent range of DVDs, CDs and a vast array of electrical goods. Digital cameras are in plentiful supply, as are camcorders. There are English-language novels to be found on the top floor, along with the excellent café (p75).

Galerie de Thézan
11 rue Maccarani (04 93 82 27 02). **Open** 11am-7pm Tue-Sat. **Map** p72 C3 ④⑦
Approaching its 25th birthday, this well-established private gallery specialises in far eastern antiquities. Expect to find statues, furniture and artefacts large and small from Tibet, Japan and China. Archaeological treasures from the Han, Ming and Tang dynasties obviously carry significant price tags, but there are other, more affordable options too. Advice is expert, service is friendly – a rare but welcome combination.

Galeries Lafayette
6 avenue Jean Médecin (04 92 17 36 36). **Open** 9am-8pm Mon-Sat. **Map** p73 D3 ④⑧
A branch of France's famous chain of department stores, this is a substantial

(six-floor) building packed to the rafters with consumer goods of all stripes. In the basement, you'll find a well-stocked food hall; on the upper floors, men's, women's and children's clobber; on the top floor, restaurant and café; and on the ground floor, the inevitable gust of perfume that greets shoppers the world over as they walk in from the street.

Nice Étoile
30 avenue Jean Médecin (04 92 17 38 17). **Open** 10am-7.30pm Mon-Sat. **Map** p72 C2 ④⑨
The city's main shopping mall, Nice Étoile is not exactly a glamorous address but it gets the job done. Organised over four floors is the usual range of fashion wear, shoe shops, sports wear and accessories outlets, plus the occasional optician and pharmacy. There's also a reasonable drycleaners in the basement, which is handy to know about.

Nicolas
23 avenue Jean Médecin (04 93 88 53 71). **Open** 9am-8pm Mon-Sat. **Map** p72 C2 ⑤⓪
With branches all over town, Nicolas provides a valuable service to wine

FNAC p82

shoppers who want more than the supermarket has to offer but want to pay less than a more serious-minded wine shop would demand. The usual range of house quaffables, plus a good selection of bottles to impress.

Paraboot
2 rue Longchamp (04 93 87 61 62).
Open noon-7pm Mon; 10am-7pm Tue,
Thur-Sat; 10am-1pm, 2-7pm Wed.
Map p72 C3 ❶
High-end men's leather footwear is Paraboot's, well, boot, with an emphasis placed on quality and workmanship. Loafers, lace-ups and sandals for summer are among the styles on show. Prices are commensurate with the products and the elegant setting on one of Nice's more chi-chi shopping streets.

Petit Bâteau
13 rue Masséna (04 93 82 05 00).
Open 10am-7pm Mon-Sat.
Map p72 C4 ❷
Now with stores in more than a dozen countries around the world, Petit Bâteau is a useful resource for those wanting to kit out their children with stylish holiday togs. This branch has all the usual range of junior chic associated with the brand.

Secrets Dessous
*4 rue Masséna (04 97 03 09 03/
www.secretsdessous.com).* **Open**
10am-7pm daily. **Map** p72 C3 ❸
There are enough silky, slinky and downright sexy bras and knickers in this smart high-street boutique to convert even the most ordinary city break into a saucy weekend. The black and scarlet Barbara range is the kind of thing that the digital camera was invented for.

Timberland
14 rue Liberté (04 93 82 12 48).
Open 10am-7pm daily. **Map** p72 C3 ❹
This wooden-fronted corner store suits Timberland's aesthetic of rugged durability down to the ground. The well-made men's clothes are in line with the brand's usual eco-tough-guy image but are also smart enough to get away with in most clubs and restaurants around these parts.

Nightlife

Le Before
18 rue du Congrès (04 93 87 85 59).
Open 6pm-12.30am Mon-Sat.
Map p72 B3 ❺

NICE & CANNES BY AREA

Your good health

Organic food is a boom industry in Nice.

Some of the finest food in the world is to be found in France. But where the gastronomic fatherland did not, until very recently, perform so well was in the arena of healthy eating. In most regions of the country, announcing to a waiter that you are vegetarian would simply have caused his lip to curl in disdain. The further clarification that this means no meat at all, not even chicken, would have induced something closer to disgust. And confessing to veganism or wheat intolerance might even have made his head explode. But the times are changing, albeit gradually. And at the forefront of this change are restaurants like Nice's **Bio et Cie** (p74).

It evolved as a kind of lifestyle statement rather than as a marketing gimmick, when the owners decided that they would introduce the rigours of their own organic and health-conscious diet to the menu of their popular New Town restaurant. And it has gone from strength to strength. Some dishes are lactose or gluten free, others use only rice flour instead of wheat; nowhere is cow's milk to be found, with cheeses made from goat's or sheep's milk. Produce is organic, with the provenance of the meat meticulously charted, and the menu changes by the day (nothing is frozen; you'll hear no ping of the microwave in this kitchen). Evening seminars followed, of course, by food are regularly timetabled.

The restaurant at super-hip Hi Hôtel, **La Cantine Bio d'Alain Alexanian** (p75) is another trailblazer in the field of organic eating, with a particularly popular Sunday brunch deal, which includes a session in the hotel's slickly appointed hammam. But the buck(wheat) doesn't stop there. A growing number of shops in Nice are also peddling a variety of blameless products, such as the organic cosmetics (Weleda, Dr Hauschka and the rest) that are the speciality at **Bérénice et Eglantine** (p65).

With doors that look like they were designed to withstand a bomb blast, Before has been designed with an industrial New York aesthetic in mind. And down in its brick cellar, the city's bright young (and not so young) things warm up for a night on the dance floor. Cocktails and an upbeat soundtrack help them get to where they're going.

Le Flag

6 rue Eugène Emmanuel (04 93 87 29 67/www.le-flag.com). **Open** 8.30pm-1am Wed, Thur; 10pm-2.30am Fri-Sun. **Map** p72 C3 **⑤⑥**
Known primarily as a gay venue, the Flag is a fun, colourful and exuberant lounge bar with a happy, clubby vibe on the weekend. Resident DJ Anorak does a good job of getting the crowd going (as do the various house cocktails – try the quietly lethal 'XY'). Deli-style snacks are available, but this is more of a sipping, lounging and late-night grooving kind of place.

Ôdace

29 rue Alphonse Karr (04 93 82 37 66/www.odaceclub.com). **Open** 11pm-5am Thur-Sat. **Map** p72 B2 **⑤⑦**
Louche orientalism emanates from every nook of this opulent nightspot.

There's a decent restaurant on the premises but the best reason to come is for the decadent party atmosphere that cooks up later on, when the DJ is getting into some deep house and the champagne-sipping clientele are getting up to dance. You can expect some big names on the decks here, from time to time.

Le Smarties

10 rue Défly (04 93 62 30 75/http:// nicesmarties.free.fr). **Open** 7pm-2am Mon, Thur-Sun. **Map** p73 E2 **⑤⑧**
Billing itself as an 'electro lounge', Smarties is a retro-hip bar populated by the kind of clientele who don't look out of place among the decor of funky divans and 1970s television sets. The decks get regular lo-fi workovers by some well-known local spinners such as International DJ Gigolo and Miss Van Der Rohe. Nice in Nice.

Arts & leisure

Acropolis

1 esplanade Kennedy (04 93 92 83 00/www.nice-acropolis.com). **Open** according to programme. **Map** p73 F1 **⑤⑨**
Some kind of special event, exhibition or a large-scale performance (ballets,

Ôdace

operas and the like) is what lures most tourists to this modern mega-structure just a few minutes walk north of Vieux Nice. Business people also converge here for all manner of conferences, conventions and shows.

La Bulle d'Isis

37 rue Masséna (04 93 87 17 13/ www.labulledisis.fr). **Open** 10am-7pm Mon-Wed, Fri, Sat. **Map** p72 C4 ⑥⓪

What 21st-century city can really feel complete until it has a spa? Fortunately for Nice, this stylish retreat ensures its citizenry don't ever get too frazzled. Many of the treatments outlined on the 80-strong menu will strike wind chimes of recognition among spa aficionados, although few could possibly be familiar with the practice of 'chococooning', of which rolling around in creamy ganache and melted chocolate is but a small part.

Cinéma Rialto

4 rue de Rivoli (04 93 88 08 41). **Open** according to programme. **Map** p72 A4 ⑥①

Five air-conditioned theatres show English-language only new releases at this comfortable, central cinema. Cheap tickets are available in the daytime, but most punters (tourists and Anglophone residents) tend to come at night.

Cinémathèque de Nice

3 esplanade de Kennedy (04 92 04 06 66/www.cinematheque-nice.com). **Open** according to programme. **Map** p73 F1 ⑥②

Good international programme of classic films. All the screenings are in *version originale* with French subtitles. Come 15 minutes early to get a seat.

Nicea Location Rent

9 avenue Thiers (04 93 82 42 71/ www.nicealocationrent.com). **Open** 10am-5pm Mon-Sat. **Map** p72 B1 ⑥③

Roll up, roll up – give your poor feet a rest and jump on one of the many types and sizes of scooter for rent at this friendly hire shop. Otherwise, step into a pair of rollerblades or on to the saddle of a push bike and leave no carbon footprint behind you.

Théâtre National de Nice

promenade des Arts (04 93 13 90 90). **Open** for shows. **Map** p73 E3 ⑥④

High-profile productions of French and foreign classics, as well as a robust programme of contemporary theatre.

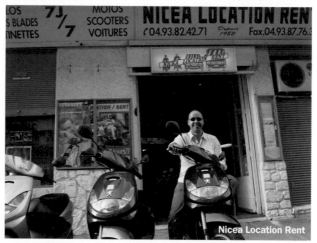

Nicea Location Rent

Promenade & the Beaches

If most of the history and character is crammed into the labyrinth of Vieux Nice, then it's here, on the sun-spangled **promenade des Anglais**, that the real action is. In-line skaters carve through the crowds, speedboats haul shrieking parascenders skywards and swarthy boys flirt with bikini-clad girls at the ice-cream stands. The bay itself is one long stripe of bleached pebble and turquoise water, divided between the volleyball courts and crisp white sun loungers of the private beaches, and the colourful melee of the public ones. And as evening falls, the promenade comes alive with sunset strollers and post-work joggers, while parents sitting on the famous blue seats watch their children devour waffles and Nutella crêpes. Until finally, when the last stragglers have packed up their towels and wandered home, the bars and restaurants get going, and the sea becomes a dark, glittering backdrop to the evening's festivities.

If you want to make the most of your sun-worshipping, it's worth taking note of how the **Baie des Anges** is divided up. Much of its steep, pebbly shoreline (remember to pack some sandals) is open to the public at all times of day, throughout the year. And it is on these **public beaches** that you can expect to encounter serious crowds in summer. If that doesn't faze you, then fine (just remember to leave any valuables at home – the normal seaside drill), but

Promenade & the Beaches

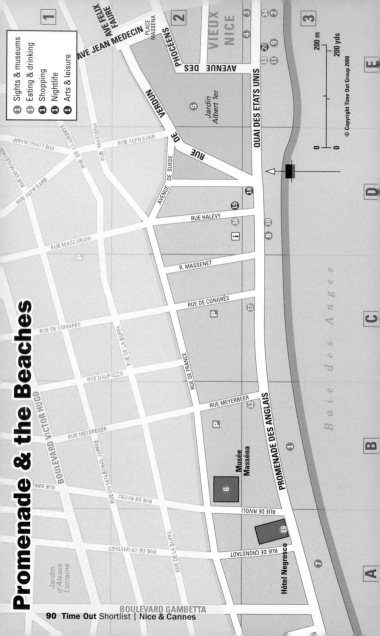

Sights & museums

Eating & drinking

Shopping

Nightlife

Arts & leisure

AVE JEAN MEDECIN

AVE FELIX FAURE

PLACE MASSENA

PHOCÉENS

VIEUX NICE

AVENUE DES

DE VERDUN

RUE ALPH KARR

RUE MASSENA

RUE DE LA LIBERTE

RUE ALPH KARR

RUE

RUE LONGCHAMP

RUE MACCARANI

AVENUE DE SUEDE

Jardin Albert 1er

QUAI DES ETATS UNIS

RUE HALEVY

R. MASSENET

RUE DE CONGRÈS

RUE DE CONGRES

RUE DE LA BUFFA

RUE DALPOZZO

RUE DE FRANCE

RUE MEYERBEER

RUE MEYERBEER

RUE DU MARECHAL JOFFRE

RUE DE RIVOLI

RUE BERL

BOULEVARD VICTOR HUGO

Jardin d'Alsace Lorraine

RUE DE LA BUFFA

RUE DE CRONSTADT

RUE DE RIVOLI

Musée Masséna

Hôtel Negresco

PROMENADE DES ANGLAIS

Baie des Anges

BOULEVARD GAMBETTA

© Copyright Time Out Group 2008

200 m

200 yds

if you'd rather occupy a more exclusive patch of sunlight, you'll need to pay the entrance fee on one of the **private beaches**. The best of these are reviewed in this chapter and, taken from east to west from the foot of the colline du Château, run as follows: Castel Plage; Opéra Plage; Plage Beau Rivage; Blue Beach; Neptune Plage.

Some of Nice's most iconic buildings are also to be found on the waterfront, such as the two hotels, the **Negresco** and the **Palais de la Méditerranée**. The **Musée d'Art et d'Histoire** at the **Palais Masséna** has been undergoing serious renovation work and was still not finished at the time of writing. For the latest information on this, contact the **Centre du Patrimoine**.

Promenade des Anglais p89

Sights, museums & beaches

Blue Beach

32 promenade des Anglais (04 93 87 10 36). **Open** *June-Sept* 8am-midnight daily. *Oct-May* 8am-7pm daily. **Sun lounger** €10. **Map** p90 B3 **1**
See box p93.

Castel Plage

8 quai des Etats-Unis (04 93 85 22 66). **Open** *Mar-Sept* 8.30am-7pm daily. Closed Oct-Feb. **Sun lounger** €14. **Map** p90 E3 **2**
See box p93.

Centre du Patrimoine

75 quai des Etats-Unis (04 92 00 41 90). **Open** 8.30am-5pm Mon-Fri. **Map** p90 E3 **3**
Nice's heritage centre seems to be right at home among the vaulted and frescoed ceilings of its new base, in one of the quai's beautifully restored 19th-century *terrasses*. The main reason to visit the centre is to take advantage of the impressive programme of guided walks, which last around two hours and cost just €3 per person. The range of topics (and areas of the town) covered by the guides is exceptional, taking in subjects as diverse as Baroque and art deco architecture, and Matisse's Nice, through to meticulous examinations of the city's botanical heritage. Guides are well informed and seem to have the ability to convey their knowledge in an animated and genuinely interesting style. Both the office and the website contain a mass of scholarly information on the city's sights, monuments, famous residents and historical highlights, as well as specialised inventories for sightseers who've seen it all.

Galerie des Ponchettes

77 quai des Etats-Unis (04 93 62 31 24). **Open** 10am-noon, 2-6pm Tue-Sat. **Admission** free. **Map** p90 E3 **4**
The history of this 19th-century building is far from arty – it has been somewhat ignominiously used in its time as a public *lavoir* and a fish market – but its conversion in the 1960s into a municipal art gallery was a stroke of genius. The vaulted interior lends itself very well to the varied mix of (mainly modern) foreign and domestic art that is

Time Out
Travel Guides

Worldwide

All our guides are
written by a team of
local experts with a
unique and stylish
insider perspective.
We offer essential tips,
trusted advice and
honest reviews for
everything you need
to know in the city.

Over 50 destinations
available at all good
bookshops and at
timeout.com/shop

Time Out
Guides

Hot rocks

The hierarchy of pebble beach.

Bale des Anges

It's worth knowing what your options are before you head down to the seashore and throw your towel in with the punters on the public beaches. For one thing, you'll not be *throwing* your towel, you'll be carefully unrolling it on one of the patches of scalding pebbles that is not yet occupied, and for another, you'll need to keep a careful eye on your gear when you go for a swim (not an easy feat when negotiating the Med's punchy little waves). Unsupervised bags are easy pickings for opportunistic thieves.

Going private can eliminate many of these hassles (lockers keep your belongings safe, thick hessian carpets lead right down to the water's edge, protecting your feet against the tricky terrain). But the options vary, and some beaches are better than others. It all depends on what you're looking for (and, of course, where you're staying, as a good many of the hotels have preferential rates with various private beaches).

Taking them in order, running east to west from the foot of the colline du Château, this is our pick of the private beaches. First up is **Castel Plage** (p91), with its smart restaurant and decking. In the lee of the headland, this beach is a wonderfully sheltered spot, with comfortable loungers and efficient waiter service. Similarly, **Opéra Plage** (p93), the next in line, offers a smart spread with the addition of a locker for valuables. But the classiest patch on this strip is the venerable **Plage Beau Rivage** (p95), with its art deco signage announcing the steps down to the blue and white livery of mattresses and umbrellas. Affiliated to the hotel of the same name, the Beau Rivage offers top-notch dining at the water's edge.

Blue Beach (p91), the only one of the bunch to be open all year round, tends to offer watersports, such as parasailing. And our final pick is **Neptune Plage** (p93), a must for Riviera purists with its picturesque wrought-iron jetty.

shown here in an ongoing programme of temporary exhibitions. The Galerie de la Marine at no.59 (04 93 91 92 90) is cast from the same mould.

Jardin Albert 1er

avenue de Verdun/avenue des Phocéens. **Open** 24hrs daily. **Map** p90 E2 ❺

A leafy link between the old and new towns, Nice's oldest public garden acts as a kind of respirator, filtering out the pollution and noise of passing traffic, and providing local residents with a shady spot to escape the heat and catch their breath. Looking around on a typical summer's morning, this would seem to be where many Niçois who either don't have or have grown tired of their own balconies come to read the paper, watch the world pass by and possibly venture a game of chess or cards. Sculptor Bernard Venet's giant steel arc, intended as a tribute to Nice's famous coastline, is the focal point of the park.

Musée d'Art et d'Histoire

Palais Masséna, 65 rue de France (04 93 91 19 10). **Open** call for details. **Map** p90 B2 ❻

Still undergoing extensive refurbishment work at the time of writing, this museum (also known as the Musée Masséna) occupies a beautiful Italianate villa built in the late 1890s for the aristocratic Victor Masséna. Much of the decor (notably in the Directoire and Empire rooms) was cannibalised from other chateaux, which have long since disappeared, making the building itself something of a historical showpiece. But the real charm of the place lies in the various artefacts on display (suits of armour, Napoleon's coronation robe and death mask), as well as the works of assorted primitive painters. Call in advance for information on new visiting hours and admission prices.

Neptune Plage

Opposite Hôtel Negresco, promenade des Anglais (04 93 87 16 60). **Open** *Mar-Nov* 8am-8pm daily. Closed Dec-Feb. **Sun lounger** €15. **Map** p90 A3 ❼
See box p93.

Nice Le Grand Tour

promenade des Anglais (04 92 29 17 00/www.nicelegrandtour.com). **Admission** €18. **Map** p90 D3 ❽

A lively commentary is piped into your ears through the stethoscope-style headphones that one always finds aboard these open-topped tour buses, while the warm Mediterranean breeze ruffles your hair (along with the occasional overhanging branch – top-deck passengers take note). The bus ventures further afield than its diminutive counterpart, le Petit Train, taking in the port and the villas in the hills beyond. A good view of the war memorial, along with sweeping vistas from some of the higher vantage points are worth the fare alone. But the hop on, hop off system, combined with the fact that the route also snakes round the Cimiez museum circuit, makes this excellent bus tour a hassle-free bet for a first look at the city.

Opéra Plage

30 quai des Etats-Unis (04 93 62 31 51). **Open** *Easter-Oct* 8.30am-sunset daily. Closed Nov-Easter. **Sun lounger** €8. **Map** p90 E3 ❾
See box p93.

Petit Train de Nice

promenade des Anglais, opposite Jardin Albert 1er (06 16 39 53 51/www.petit trainnice.com). **Admission** €6.50. **Map** p90 D3 ❿

As cheesy as these miniature train rides can undoubtedly be, this particular example is actually quite good fun. Yes, you're bimbling along in a motorised toy-town train, but the route itself soon eclipses any sense of self-consciousness, as you wind up through the picturesque streets of the old town towards the colline du Château and back down again to the seafront. Hop on and off at the designated stops.

Plage Beau Rivage

107 quai des Etats-Unis (04 92 47 82 82/www.nicebeaurivage.com). **Open** *Apr-Oct* 9am-11pm daily. Closed Nov-Mar. **Sun lounger** €13. **Map** p90 E3 ⓫
See box p93.

Beau Rivage (Plage)

Eating & drinking

11e Art

11 rue Meyerbeer (04 93 87 57 15).
Open noon-2.30pm, 6-11pm Tue-Sun.
€€. Global. Map p90 B3 ⑫
Very much situated in the vanguard of
Nice's new wave of casual, lounge-style
restaurants, 11e Art provides a sophisticated menu of global dishes, with a
particular focus on eastern flavours
(one of the chefs is Japanese). The background music is audible enough to register as a slick counterpoint to the
evening's conversation, but not loud
enough to drown it out.

Beau Rivage (Plage)

*107 quai des Etats-Unis (04 92 47 82
82/www.nicebeaurivage.com).* **Open**
Apr-Oct noon-2.30pm, 7-10pm daily.
Closed Nov-Mar. **€€. Brasserie.**
Map p90 E3 ⑬
Its wooden decking rising gracefully
above the shingle of Baie des Anges,
the Beau Rivage's linen-clad tables are
situated just yards from the clear, blue
waters of the Mediterranean. A good
steak, fresh fish or a bowl of pasta are
the kind of wholesome staples that you
can expect to find on the menu here.
And if you come on a Sunday or
Monday night, you might even get to
hear some live jazz with your meal.

Le Castel

*8 quai des Etats-Unis (04 93 85 22
66).* **Open** *Apr-Oct* noon-2.30pm,
7-10pm daily. Closed Nov-Mar. **€€.**
Brasserie. Map p90 E3 ⑭
At the far eastern end of the Baie des
Anges, Le Castel beach restaurant is
the ideal place to surf a long lunch hour
far into the afternoon. Take a table on
the decking, order from the very
respectable *carte* and survey the
bronzed bodies and azure Med with a
glass of ice-cold rosé in your hand.

Le Chantecler

*Hôtel Negresco, 37 promenade des
Anglais (04 93 16 64 00).* **Open**
12.30-2pm, 8-10pm daily. Closed Jan.
€€€€. Haute cuisine.
Map p90 A3 ⑮
The city's hot toque is now crowning
the head of culinary wunderkind Jean-
Denis Rieubland, who has replaced
Bruno Turbot in the Negresco's flagship kitchen. Expect a sophisticated
take on traditional provençal flavours,
but with an accompanying price tag
that is not quite so traditional. But
unlike some of its more modern rivals,
the Chantecler simply exudes style,
from the moment you are ushered into
its wood-panelled dining room right
through to your last sip of vintage
armagnac. Pure class all the way.

Le Keep in Touch

5 rue Halévy (04 93 87 07 04).
Open 10am-2.30am Mon-Fri; 6pm-
2.30am Sat, Sun. **€€. Global.**
Map p90 D2 ⑯
Putting aside for a moment its question-
able nomenclature (most people seem
to know it simply as 'Le Keep'), this
funky, friendly and fun restaurant-cum-
bar has abandoned its former pitta-
bread with fillings concept in favour of
something more traditional. It's nothing show-stopping, but the tapas, salads and light bites keep an evening of
drinking and chatting chugging along.

Le Padouk

*13-15 promenade des Anglais (04 92
14 77 00/www.concorde-hotels.com).*
Open noon-2.30pm, 7-10pm Tue-Sat.
€€€€. Haute cuisine.
Map p90 C3 ⑰
Replacing the much-revered Bruno
Sohn in the kitchen at this palatial hotel
restaurant can't have been easy, but
new arrival Philippe Thomas seems to
be making a good job of it. His menu
features dishes like roasted fish of the
day with stuffed fennel and anis reduction or trio of suckling lamb with ricot-
ta-stuffed courgette flowers. Otherwise,
things remain much as they were
before, with a moneyed clientele filling
the sophisticated wood-panelled dining
room with discreet conversation.

Nightlife

Casino Ruhl

*1 promenade des Anglais (04 97 03 12
33).* **Open** 10am-4am Mon-Fri; 10am-
5am Fri-Sun. **Map** p90 D3 ⑱
Modern, sprawling and packed, Casino
Ruhl dabbles in a bit of everything.
There's a sea of slot machines and
video poker (some 300, in fact), as well
as roulette, card tables (blackjack, stud
poker), restaurants, regular cabarets
and revues. You'll run out of cash
before you run out of things to do.

Le Klub

*6 rue Halévy (04 93 16 27 56/www.
leklub.net).* **Open** midnight-5am Wed-
Sun. **Map** p90 D2 ⑲
The city's premier gay nightspot, but
clubbers of all orientations are welcome
to come and hear the best DJ line-up on
the Riviera, with everyone from upcoming local spinners to names like Jeff
Mills manning the decks.

Arts & leisure

Roller Station

*49 quai des États-Unis (04 93 62 99
05/www.roller-station.com).* **Open** Apr-
Sept 9.30am-8pm daily. Oct-Mar 10am-
6.30pm. **Map** p90 E3 ⑳
In-line skates and bikes of all types for
hire, plus Crocs sandals to buy.

Casino Ruhl

Roll with it

See the sights on skates.

You'll see them zipping past, missing you and the others by a matter of a few carefully judged centimetres, usually bare-torsoed men and bikini-clad women, toned and tanned. These are the in-line skaters. An indigenous breed of poseur on wheels, part human, part vehicle, part iPod. And then there are the others, the nocturnal variety, who surface much more timidly and far less frequently. They move in packs, some gliding away with practised ease, others clinging together, to railings, to benches and even to passing strangers as they wobble uncertainly into the night. This is **Nice Roller Attitude** (06 09 07 57 19, www.nice-roller-attitude.com), and for one night a month, they rule the roads. The motorway is closed to traffic, the shops are boarded up, right-minded citizens scurry indoors, and the assembled mass of locals, tourists, and assorted skaters of all shapes and sizes take to the streets.

The name of the outing is 'Nice by Night' and it takes place on the second Friday of every month. All you need is a pair of skates (rentals from **Roller Station**) and the right 'roller attitude' – meaning a willingness to give it a go and have a laugh. The rendez-vous is at 9pm next to the sign announcing Plage Beau Rivage on quai des Etats-Unis. The route is a pretty straightforward skate up towards the motorway and back, sticking to the wider, easier roads (from which traffic is diverted by the local gendarmes).

Sound too easy? Then try the club's more specialised monthly outing through the busy streets of Vieux Nice, where there are a good many obstacles to be avoided. This is a trickier route and is open only to those who have cut their teeth as urban skaters. This outing takes place every Friday, same time, same starting point as 'Nice by Night'. Both events are free, fun and always festive.

Port & Around

With far fewer hotels than the New Town or even hotel-poor Vieux Nice, the Port is an area where most visitors lodge aboard ships. But if that conjures an image of salty seafarers, nothing could be further from the truth. The yachts and gin palaces moored in Nice's harbour are smart, shiny and staffed by liveried crews. Some of the busts might be enhanced with silicone, but the Guccis, Rolexes and Prada swimsuits are all real.

Happily, though, you don't need to be part of the yachty clique to fit in on the dock of the bay, where most of the bars and restaurants are down-to-earth locals' haunts (with the occasional, very fancy exception – hey, a billionaire's gotta eat). And just wandering around the streets here, there is a sense of a city going about its business, unlike in the more overtly touristy Vieux Nice where the prevailing tone is more of a city made into a business.

That said, it's still only a short walk around the headland to get to the promenade des Anglais, with the splendid **War Memorial** and the magnificent views from Pointe Rauba Capeu en route. Or else wend your way past the antiques shops of rue Catherine Ségurane and take the back way into town (stopping for a sweet treat at **Confiserie Florian** and a quick shufti at the **Puces de Nice** along the way).

Sights & museums

Jardin Vigier
boulevard Franck (08 92 70 74 07).
Open *Apr, May, Sept* 8am-7pm daily.
June-Aug 8am-8pm daily. *Oct-Mar*
8am-6pm daily. **Admission** free.
Map p99 C5 ❶

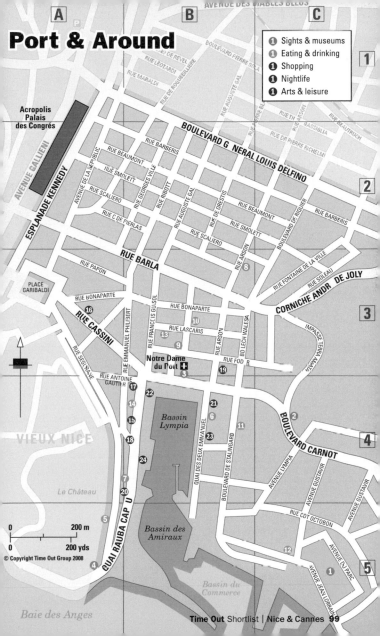

Port & Around

Acropolis Palais des Congrés

❶	Sights & museums
❶	Eating & drinking
❶	Shopping
❶	Nightlife
❶	Arts & leisure

AVENUE DES DIABLES BLEUS

BOULEVARD PIERRE SOLA

RUE DE REVEL
RUE LÉOTARDI
RUE MARALDI
RUE DE ROQUEBILLIÈRE
RUE AUGUSTE GAL
RUE TH ARSON
RUE CASSIGLIA
RUE DR PIERRE RICHELMI
RUE BEAUTRUCH

BOULEVARD G NERAL LOUIS DELFINO

RUE BARBERIS
RUE BEAUMONT
RUE DE LA REPUBLIC
RUE SMOLETT
AVENUE DE LA REPUBLIC
RUE SCALIERO
RUE GEORGES VILLE
RUE RIBOTT
RUE AUGUSTE GAL
RUE DE ORESTIS
RUE BEAUMONT
RUE BARBERIS
RUE C DE PIERLAS
RUE SMOLETT
RUE SCALIERO
BOULEVARD DE RIQUIER

ESPLANADE KENNEDY
AVENUE GALLIENI

RUE BARLA
RUE ARSON ❽

RUE PAPON
RUE FONTAINE DE LA VILLE
RUE SOLEAU

PLACE GARIBALDI
CORNICHE ANDR DE JOLY
RUE BONAPARTE
RUE BONAPARTE

RUE CASSINI ❶⑥
RUE FRANCIS GUISOL
RUE LASCARIS ❶⓪
RUE SEBASTIANE
RUE EMMANUEL PHILIBERT
❶③
❾
RUE ARSON
BD LECH WALESA
IMPASSE TERRA AMARA

RUE ANTOINE GAUTIER
❶⑦
Notre Dame du Port ✝ ❸
RUE FOD R
❶⑨

❶④
❷②
Bassin Lympia
❷①
❻
❷③
❶①
BOULEVARD CARNOT ❷
❶⑤
❶⑧
QUAI DES DEUX EMMANUEL
❷④
BOULEVARD DE STALINGRAD
AVENUE LYMPIA
AVENUE GUSTAVIR
AVENUE GUSTAVIR

VIEUX NICE

Le Château
QUAI RAUBA CAP U
❼
❷⓪
RUE CDT OCTOBON

❺
Bassin des Amiraux
AVENUE JEAN LORRAIN
AVENUE N PARC
❶②
❶

0   200 m
0   200 yds
© Copyright Time Out Group 2008

❹
Bassin du Commerce

Baie des Anges

A   B   C
1   2   3   4   5

Le Bistrot du Port p102

Fastidiously maintained and, even to the non-horticulturalist, a pleasant prospect, this showpiece park is where the renowned Phoenix canariensis (Canary Island date palm) was acclimatised to the Riviera in 1864. The eponymous Viscount de Vigier introduced this species of palm (which has since become a symbol of the region) and it now stands alongside some far rarer examples of the genus, such as the Livistona australis (cabbage tree palm). But if botany isn't your thing, that shouldn't diminish the simple enjoyment of the serene and shady corners to be found in these landscaped gardens, where many locals come simply to walk their dogs, wag their chins and stretch their legs.

Musée de Paléontologie Humaine de Terra Amata

25 boulevard Carnot (04 93 55 59 93/ www.musee-terra-amata.org). **Open** 10am-6pm Tue-Sun. **Admission** €4. **Map** p99 C4 ❷

Constructed on the site of a prehistoric settlement… If this sounds like the beginning of a Stephen King novel, fear not, the outcome here is guaranteed to be wholly benign. An investigation into life on the Riviera 400,000 years ago, the Terra Amata makes use of a variety of prehistoric artefacts to answer the question emblazoned across one of its walls: 'where do we come from?' A human footprint in limestone, a cave encampment and crude stone tools are just a few of the clues that our hirsute forebears left scattered behind them.

Notre Dame du Port

8 place Ile de Beauté (04 93 89 53 05). **Open** 9am-noon, 3-6pm daily. **Admission** free. **Map** p99 B3 ❸

Depending on when you catch it, this venerable old church can be a charming sight or a rather depressing spectacle. The latter situation is caused by the colony of dead-end drunks who seem to favour the church steps as the stage for their gaudy opera of shouting and stupefied sprawling. On a good day, though, it's easy to see why its imposing colonnaded façade has instilled hope in the heart of many a departing seafarer and given comfort to the widows of ships that never returned. The church, known locally as the 'Immaculate Conception', has a portico featuring a beautiful statue of the Virgin Mary, who smiles tolerantly down on our mortal souls.

War Memorial

place Guynemer. **Map** p99 A5 ❹
Overlooking the sea from its vantage point just off quai Rauba Capeu, this imposing war memorial has been quarried into the southern face of the Colline du Château to commemorate the sacrifices made by local citizens during the two world wars. The structure itself is that of an art deco temple, the walls of which are tightly packed with the inscribed names of '*les fils morts*'. It is also worth noting that, diagonally across from the memorial, are some steps leading down to a bathing area on the seaward side of the harbour wall. Far less crowded than the public beaches, these massive barrage boulders provide level sunbathing platforms with panoramic views of the bay. At the eastern end, there is a small ladder to help you scramble down into the deep, crystal clear water.

Eating & drinking

L'Allegro

6 place Guynemar (04 93 56 62 06).
Open noon-1.45pm, 8-10pm Mon-Fri; 8-10pm Sat. €€. **Italian**. Closed Aug.
Map p99 A5 ❺
A troupe of frescoed commedia dell'arte characters surveys the mealtime crowds at this lovably straightforward Italian. The delicious, freshly made pasta dishes, risottos and skilfully cooked tratt classics have garnered quite a following, so it's always worth booking in advance.

L'Âne Rouge

7 quai des deux Emmanuel (04 93 89 49 63/www.anerougenice.com).
Open noon-2pm, 7-10pm Mon, Tue, Fri-Sun; 7-10pm Thur. €€. **Fish**.
Map p99 B4 ❻

Stick your oar in

Kayaking up the coast is Nice's latest craze.

Boat trips are all very well but if you really want to get up close and personal with nature, then get into a sea kayak and start paddling. Or at least, that's what Aymeri, owner of kayak and raft company **Les Eskimos à L'Eau** (www.eskimosaleau.com, 06 11 38 02 82), fervently believes. And, to be honest, once you've tried it, it's hard to disagree.

Trips, departing from a prearranged point at Nice's port (just call Aymeri and he'll come down to meet you), start from around €40 per head. The format is flexible but the most common arrangement is either for a full-day or morning package. Leaving from the harbour, the route follows the curve of the promenade des Anglais, making a landfall around noon for a picnic lunch.

'The extent of the trip depends very much on the capabilities of those taking part,' explains Aymeri. 'I can adapt myself to a properly physical outing or to a gentle paddle – it's led by the customer.' Which is good news, as many first-timers are shocked by how physically challenging sea kayaking is. You can expect to sleep well the following night.

For the truly intrepid, Aymeri offers the chance to join him down the coast in Cannes and paddle out to the islands, or else to meet at one of a number of inland train stations to shoot the rapids of the Var in a range of inflatable rafts.

Widely regarded as one of the best seafood restaurants in Nice, L'Âne Rouge enjoys a suitably nautical location right on the harbour's edge. As a result, the food could only be fresher if you caught it yourself. Fish is delivered daily, vegetables are grown nearby and the delicate dishes that chef Michel Devillers creates from these ingredients are mouth-watering. (Sautéed sea bream with onion chutney and artichokes *à la barigoule* being a typical example.) And for those who might pale at the prices, there's a bistro version a few doors along at sister restaurant Bistrot Canaille Hit.

Le Bistrot du Port

28 quai Lunel (04 93 55 21 70).
Open noon-2pm, 7-10pm Mon, Thur-Sun; noon-2pm Tue. €€. **French**.
Map p99 B4 ❼
Looking out on to the gin palaces and luxury yachts of Nice's old port, this bright yellow bistro has great food, fine wines and excellent service. Last time we ate there, the chef recommended that our party share a sea bass freshly caught that day, which he roasted in a salt crust and served with a drizzle of first-rate olive oil. Unforgettable.

Boni

66 rue Arson (04 93 56 27 46). **Open** noon-2.30pm, 7-10pm Tue-Sat. €€.
Italian. Map p99 B3 ❽
So successful was the first Boni (on rue Barla) that they decided to experiment with this outpost, offering the same easy-going formula of affordable pasta and Piedmontese specialities, coupled with decent wine and friendly, efficient service. The decor is modern and sophisticated, with a fine chandelier setting the discreetly glamorous tone.

Café Borghese

9 rue Fodéré (04 92 04 83 83).
Open 8am-midnight Mon-Sat.
€€. **Brasserie**. Map p99 B3 ❾
In the shadow of the imposing Notre Dame du Port, this friendly, easy-going bar has a cosy, intimate vibe. The terrace is a good place to watch people walk briskly by as they head towards the port and Vieux Nice. Decent food, too, if your *apéro* makes you peckish.

Chez Pipo

13 Rue Bavastro (04 93 55 88 82).
Open *Oct-June* 5.30-10pm Tue-Sun.
July, Aug 5.30-10pm Mon-Fri, Sun. €.
Pizza/socca. Map p99 B3 ❿

Zucca Magica p104

Come here early and expect to wait because, whatever the time, you can be guaranteed that Chez Pipo will be absolutely rammed. Socca specialists, pizza geniuses, *pissaladière* perfectionists – these boys are churning out addictively delicious food day in, day out. Bring a friend, bring a spouse, bring whoever you like, but if there's only one seat free, drop them like a stone.

Les Pins d'Alep
40 boulevard Stalingrad (04 93 26 18 50) **Open** noon-2pm, 7.30-10pm Mon, Tue, Thur-Sat. Closed Nov-Jan. **€. Middle Eastern**. Map p99 B4 ⓫
A *traiteur* as well as a restaurant (it's hard to leave empty-handed, as you pass the display of houmous, *baba ganoush* and other deli treats), Les Pins brings an authentic taste of the farther shores of the Mediterranean to these European climes. Influences from Armenia to the owners' native Syria are present on the menu, with comfortingly familiar cameos from the mous sakas, kebabs and baklavas of this world. The short list of Lebanese wines is more of an afterthought – this is, first and foremost, somewhere to enjoy some genuinely tasty home cooking.

La Réserve
60 boulevard Franck Pilatte (04 97 08 14 80/04 97 08 29 98/www. jouni.fr). **Open** *Bistro* noon-10pm daily. *Restaurant* noon-2pm, 7-10pm Tue-Sat. **€€** Bistro. **€€€** Restaurant. **French/Haute cuisine**. Map p99 C5 ⓬
This iconic building, unoccupied for more than a decade, has been brought to life again by stellar chef Jouni Tormanen, who moved his whole operation here in spring 2007. A turret-like structure on a rocky outcrop, flanked by a picturesque diving platform, La Réserve is a belle époque monument, into which a prosthesis of bistro, bar and fine-dining restaurant (L'Atelier du Goût) has been inserted. The result: a slick, quietly glamorous operation. The spirit of the menu remains unchanged from the days when Jouni's Atelier was set in a less glamorous location, with dishes like the signature open ravioli of *homard bleu* setting off the culinary fireworks. The bistro's menu roves a little more widely, offering miso soup in the same breath as rabbit confit or a good risotto, and tends not to eat into your holiday money with the same man sized bites as the carte upstairs.

Trattoria de Giuseppe

10 rue Lascaris (no phone). **Open**
8-11pm Tue-Sat. **€€**. No credit cards.
Italian. Map p99 B3 ⓭
They don't make it easy for you to dine
at this superb portside local (the
absence of a phone means you need to
turn up and take pot luck), but if that
doesn't put you off, you should be in
for a treat. Good-quality *cucina* takes
the form of silky risottos, al dente pasta
dishes and regional specialities. Just
see what's on offer when you get there,
and take a chance on something you've
not tried before. Odds on, it'll be good.
Just one word of warning, though: the
house red is cheap for a reason.

Zucca Magica

4 bis quai Papacino (04 93 56 25 27).
Open 12.30-2pm, 7-9.30pm Tue-Sat.
€€. No credit cards. **Vegetarian**.
Map p99 B4 ⓮
Hallowe'en lasts all year round at this
extraordinary vegetarian restaurant,
where the pumpkin is king of the menu
and the candlelit interior (not to mention the larger than life, bearded owner)
looks like something out of a fairy tale.
The eponymous gourd comes in every
guise from stews to pasta to dessert. A
good laugh, with good food thrown in
at more than fair prices.

Shopping

Confiserie Florian

14 quai Papacino (04 93 55 43 50).
Open 9am-noon, 2-6.30pm daily.
Map p99 B4 ⓯
The vast copper pots and jam-making
paraphernalia are on display for all to
see in the kitchens of this niçois institution. In addition to its famous jams
and preserves, Florian produces all
kinds of sweets and syrups, as well as
an aperitif and a liqueur.

Fun 'n Roll

*13 rue Cassini (04 93 55 12 32/
www.fun-n-roll.com).* **Open** 9.30am-
7pm Mon-Sat. Map p99 A3 ⓰
In-line and roller skates, skateboards
and scooters to buy, or hire from the
reasonable price of €6 per day.

Georges Manuelian

*8 rue Antoine Gautier (06 08 07
26 97).* **Open** 10am-5pm Tue-Sat.
Map p99 B4 ⓱
Of all the many antiques shops that
famously line rue Antoine Gautier, we
rate this warehouse of collectibles as
the most fun to explore. Unlike some of
its snootier neighbours, Georges
Manuelian contains much that even
fairly normal people might imagine
having in their homes. If not a chandelier or a pair of 1920s armchairs, then
a desk ornament or a gilt mirror.

Les Puces de Nice

*place Robilante, Vieux Port (no
phone).* **Open** 10am-6pm Tue-Sat.
Map p99 B4 ⓲
Get your fingers dusty at this wonderful cluster of second-hand furniture
and bric-a-brac shops. It's the kind of
place you come to looking for a living-
room lamp and walk away from with
a Chinese fan, a statue for the garden
and an encyclopaedia of mushrooms.

Tyche Valerie

6 rue Arson (04 93 89 51 83).
Open 10am-5pm Tue-Sat. Map
p99 B3 ⓳
Ladies, forgotten your cozzie, or just
feeling a little less glam than the other
sunseekers on the beach? Then you've
come to the right place. All the bikinis
and swimsuits are made on site (the
workshop's next door) and there's a
large range of styles. Cheap it ain't but
you are getting what you pay for.

Nightlife

Blue Moon

26 quai Lunel (no phone). **Open**
11pm-5am Wed-Sat. Map p99 B4 ⓴
It can get properly hot and sweaty in
this fun-loving (if not especially pretty)
little club. On the right night, funky,
happy house music whips the crowd
into a post-bar frenzy and you can find
yourself at the heart of the most down-
to-earth and raucous party to be found
anywhere on the Riviera. Just check the
flyers to make sure you're planning to
go at the right time.

Guest

5 quai des Deux Emmanuel (04 93 56 83 83). Open 11pm-5am Wed-Sat. **Map** p99 B4 ㉑

You'll need to dress up a bit if you don't want to feel like the poor relation of the tanned, blinged-up crowd who have made Guest their club of choice. It's more of a cocktails and champagne scene than a vodka Red Bulls, dancing-on-the-bar kind of joint. But that's not to say it doesn't hot up most nights in summer and on weekends year round, when even the beautiful people blow off a bit of steam. Good, housey beats get the Prada posse dancing.

Arts & leisure

Moorings

10 quai Papacino (04 92 00 42 73/ www.moorings.fr). Open 10am-5pm Tue-Sat. **Map** p99 B4 ㉒

The Riviera outpost of a global chain, Moorings can provide yacht charter for periods as short as two days, or alternatively supply boats for longer trips up and down the coast. The office is right on the harbour, so you'll be able to see what you're getting before you sign away your money.

Nice Diving

14 quai des Docks (04 93 89 42 44/ www.nicediving.com). Open Excursions 9am-noon, 2-5pm daily. **Map** p99 B4 ㉓

The team at this highly professional scuba school attend to the needs of experienced divers and novices alike. So whether you wish to explore the coast under water, or merely want someone to tell you which end of a snorkel to suck, they'll get you aboard the boat and deal with the rest. Expect first-timer tarifs, ten-dive deals and all the options in between. The full range of equipment is available for hire – all you need to bring is a cozzie and your Jacques Cousteau alter ego.

Poseidon

quai Lunel (04 92 00 43 86/www. poseidon-nice.com). Open May-Oct 9am-2.30pm daily. *Apr, Nov* 9am-2.30pm Sat. Closed Dec-Mar. **Map** p99 B4 ㉔

Well-qualified submariners and complete novices will both find something to suit their ambitions and abilities at this catch-all centre for diving and snorkelling trips. PADI courses are available, as are the '*plongée enfants*' (kids' snorkelling) and '*baptême découverte*' (for adult first-timers) packages.

Confiserie Florian

NICE & CANNES BY AREA

Musée Archéologique de Nice-Cimiez

Cimiez & Neighbourhood Nice

Just like any other lively, sprawling city, Nice cannot be tidily summed up in a few chapters. There is no one area that contains all the best sights, the greatest museums and coolest clubs. You're going to have to walk a bit, bus a bit and stop for a fair few cool lemonades along the way if you want to really see the sights.

The beautiful residential neighbourhood of Cimiez, quietly drowsing on its hillside a few miles above Vieux Nice, is where you'll find some of the best museums in town. The dynamic duo of **Musée Matisse** and **Musée National Message Biblique Marc Chagall** draw huge crowds, while the rather more erudite **L'Eglise et Le Monastère Notre Dame de Cimiez** and **Musée Archéologique de Nice-Cimiez** offer a little more breathing space.

Further afield, **Cathédrale Saint Nicolas** (popularly known as 'the Russian church') is gobsmackingly beautiful, while the far-flung **Musée des Arts Asiatiques** and neighbouring **Parc Floral Phoenix** are only a ten-minute bus or cab ride from the pavements of the old town, and yet a world apart from its bustle and heat. The excellent **Musée des Beaux-Arts** is accessible by foot (for those who have the puff for the steep Baumettes), and be comforted

off and, once inside, the visual feast continues with a beautiful iconostasis, augmented by a huge number of intricate carvings and frescoes. Dating from the early decades of the 20th century, the interior captures a lost epoch of Russian splendour personified by Tsar Nicolas II, under whose patronage the cathedral was built. A dress code, excluding shorts, short skirts and T-shirts, is strictly enforced.

L'Eglise et Le Monastère Notre Dame de Cimiez

place du Monastère (04 93 81 00 04).
Open *Church* 9am-noon, 2-6pm daily.
Museum 10am-noon, 3-6pm Mon-Sat.
Admission free.
The church itself, which is unremarkable save for its triptych of Louis Bréa altarpieces, is not the best reason to visit this small complex affiliated to the adjoining monastery. More interesting are the muralled cloisters next door and the intriguing Musée Fransiscan, where the agonising deaths of monastic martyrs are documented. The monastery's gardens are a paradisiacal enclave of shaded cypress walkways and fragrant arbours, offering a wonderful view of the city's coastline and rooftops. In the cemetery next door, the graves of Matisse and Raoul Dufy gaze out over the same panorama.

Musée Archéologique de Nice-Cimiez

160 avenue des Arènes (04 93 81 59 57). **Open** 10am-6pm Mon, Wed Sun.
Admission €4.
The smart, well curated museum of archaeology devotes two floors of open-plan exhibition space to a dazzling array of ceramics, coinage and assorted weaponry that traces a timeline through Nice's history from 1100 BC to the Middle Ages. Outside, you'll find ancient history on a larger, less polished scale, in the form of the first-to fourth-century ruins of Cemenelum. Here, the remnants of Roman public baths and a system of paved streets are dominated by the more imposing (and still easily discernible) vestiges of a

that at the end of the trek to **Villa Arson**, you'll find not only an impressive stash of contemporary art but a first-rate café to boot. And on the subject of food, the views from **Coco Beach** restaurant are not only the most extraordinary in Nice but arguably some of the most exquisite to be found in all of France. A grand statement? Go judge for yourself.

Sights & museums

Cathédrale Saint Nicolas (Eglise Russe)

avenue Nicolas II (04 93 96 88 02).
Open *May-Oct* 9am-noon, 2.30-6pm daily. *Nov-Apr* 9.30am-noon, 2.30-5.30pm daily. **Admission** €3.
One of the most striking examples of Russian Orthodox architecture outside Russia, this cathedral is a wonderfully incongruous addition to Nice's pantheon of churches. Its five brilliantly coloured, onion-domed cupolas announce its presence from some way

400-seat amphitheatre. This latter has now been given the thumbs-up as a venue for the Nice Jazz Festival.

Musée des Arts Asiatiques

405 promenade des Anglais (04 92 29 37 00/www.arts-asiatiques.com). **Open** 10am-5pm Mon, Wed-Sun. **Admission** €4.

With a content as deliberately minimal as the architecture of the building that houses it (a wonderfully light, white marble edifice designed by Kenzo Tange), this fascinating collection is a delight to explore. Divided into geographical and historical slices of Asian and Indian history, the museum's exhibits have been carefully selected by a team of knowledgeable curators. Each exhibition space contains only a handful of artefacts (ornate mouldings from a temple, perhaps, an intricate fan or a splendid kimono), the intention being to prevent visitors from reaching saturation point too quickly. And it works. It is easy to linger in the imaginatively organised exhibition spaces, appreciating not only the objects in front of you but also how they have been positioned in the room. The equally beautiful café also offers traditional tea ceremonies on various days – call or consult the website for details.

Musée des Beaux-Arts

33 avenue des Baumettes (04 92 15 28 28/www.musee-beaux-arts-nice.org). **Open** 10am-6pm Tue-Sun. **Admission** €4.

On a hot day, it can be an uphill struggle getting to this picturesque museum, but it's worth every step. The former residence of a Ukrainian princess, the building itself is a work of art, but the real treasures are to be found within, distributed among its palatial rooms. Some of the jewels of the collection are missing following a dramatic daylight robbery in August 2007, during which paintings by Breughel, Monet and Sisley were snatched, but the scope and calibre of what remains is nonetheless impressive. The chronology ranges from 15th-century altar pieces through 18th-century greats like Fragonard to some wonderful Impressionist paintings and Rodin's imposing sculpture, *The Kiss*, which overlooks an ornate marble staircase. It's all very grand, and yet at the same time refreshingly low key. Be sure to have a little stroll in the gardens afterwards.

Musée International d'Art Naïf Anatole Jakovsky

Château Ste-Hélène, avenue de Fabron (04 93 71 78 33). **Open** 10am-6pm Mon, Wed-Sun. **Admission** €4.

A splendid pink villa houses this collection of naïve art, bequeathed to the city by the eponymous M Jakovsky. Some 600 paintings, drawings and sculptures trace the history of this artistic movement from the 18th century to the present day. Even those not naturally drawn to the style will find much to enjoy here, from the wonderful simplicity of Henri Rousseau's *Portrait de Frumence Biche en civil* through to far more elaborate paintings, such as Louis Vivin's *La Conciergerie*.

Musée Matisse

164 avenue des Arènes (04 93 81 08 08/www.musee-matisse-nice.org). **Open** 10am-6pm Mon, Wed-Sun. **Admission** €4.

Just a few steps away from the Hotel Regina, where Matisse lived, this Genoese-style 17th-century villa keeps a significant number of the artist's paintings, hundreds of his drawings and engravings, as well as an assortment of his sculptures and illustrated books. Various photographs and artefacts from Matisse's personal collection are also scattered around, giving each space a lived-in feel that is entirely in keeping with the breezy Mediterranean vibe of the villa's burnt-red façade and tall shuttered windows. From the vast cut-out *Fleurs et Fruits* in the museum's light-filled atrium to the supreme delicacy of such paintings as *Tempête à Nice*, the breadth of Matisse's output is made abundantly clear in the progression of each display.

Cathédrale Saint Nicolas (Eglise Russe) p107

NICE & CANNES BY AREA

Musée National Message Biblique Marc Chagall

avenue du Dr Ménard (04 93 53 87 20/ www.musee-chagall.fr). **Open** 10am-6pm daily. **Admission** €4.

Contained within the strict geometry of this bunker-like building (designed by Le Corbusier collaborator André Hermant) is the complete set of biblical paintings by Belarusian painter and long-time Riviera resident Marc Chagall. The thematic thread that binds together these vivid canvases is Chagall's interpretation of various episodes from three Old Testament books: the Song of Songs, Genesis and Exodus. Arresting, colourful and otherworldly, these imposing paintings are complemented by the various preparatory sketches made by the artist at the inception of this series, which was designed to transmit, in his own words, 'a certain peace, a certain sense of religion and a sense of life's meaning'. First-rate temporary exhibitions, such as 2007's critically acclaimed 'Monsters, Chimeras and Hybrids', flesh out other aspects of Chagall's formidable oeuvre. A beautiful amphitheatre at the back of the museum holds small-scale acoustic concerts against a backdrop of blue stained glass designed specifically for the venue by Chagall himself.

Observatoire de Nice

boulevard de l'Observatoire (04 92 00 30 11/ www.obs-azur.fr). **Open** *Astronomy tour* 3pm Wed, Sat. *Nature tour* 9.45am Wed; 2.15 pm Sat. **Admission** €5.

It's a fair old schlep to the summit of Mont Gros but this world-renowned observatory and architectural treasure is well worth the journey. Designed and engineered by the dynamic duo of Charles Garnier and Gustav Eiffel, the campus of 15 buildings is distributed around sprawling mountaintop grounds. It is now, first and foremost, an academic institution, joined with similar facilities across the world in ambitious projects of stellar research. However, guided tours do take place

once a week, departing from the observatory's main entrance: the 'astronomy tour' comprises a complete tour of the facility, including the enormous 18-metre (59-foot) lens; the 'nature tour' takes in the impressive array of flora and fauna in the surrounding parkland.

Parc Floral Phoenix

405 promenade des Anglais (04 92 29 77 00). Bus 9, 10, 13. **Open** *Apr-Sept* 9.30am-7.30pm daily. *Oct-Mar* 9.30am-6pm. **Admission** €2.

Just a short distance from the airport and bang next door to the Musée des Arts Asiatiques, this lush expanse of beautifully preserved Mediterranean flora is also home to a large population of local birdlife. Rare species of duck, black swans and pelicans have made their home on the shores of the park's lake, while more than 2,500 species of indigenous plants spread through its 20 separate gardens. The enormous 'green diamond', one of Europe's largest glasshouses, provides a range of suitably steamy habitats for a wide variety of tropical and subtropical plants, exquisitely delicate orchids and flora from equatorial rainforests. Temporary themes and exhibitions cover a range of topics from spiders to sculpture, while strictly ecological issues are screened (in the form of a rolling programme of documentaries) and debated every month at the *'soirée environnement'*. Entry to the screenings is free (for details, call 04 93 55 33 33).

Prieuré du Vieux Logis

59 avenue Saint Barthélémy (04 97 13 34 15). Bus 5. **Open** *Tours* June-Sept 5pm Sat; Oct-May 3pm Sat. **Admission** €3.

Meet just around the corner, in front of Saint Barthélémy church (11 montée Claire Virenque), to join up with the guided tour that visits this quirky and atmospheric villa. Remodelled in the 1930s, the building has many interesting architectural features and is also home to a collection of artworks spanning the 14th to 17th centuries. Religious art is the bag here; see for a

Lost art

Daylight robbery at the Musée des Beaux-Arts.

On Sunday 5 August 2007, what began like an ordinary weekend shift for staff at the **Musée des Beaux-Arts** (p108) was suddenly transformed into a scene straight out of a Tarantino movie. In broad daylight, a gang of five men wearing masks and jumpsuits carried out one of the most audacious art heists of recent times. Before they could work out what was happening, staff were being held at gunpoint while the gang snatched four world-famous paintings from the walls. Minutes later, the thieves vanished, as quickly as they had appeared, clutching two Breughels, a Monet and a Sisley, worth an estimated €1m. And yet, as dramatic (and traumatic) as that incident undoubtedly was, it is just the beginning of the story.

It turns out that both the Monet (*Les Falaises Près de Dieppe*) and the Sisley (*Allé de Peupliers de Moret*) had been stolen before, and what's more, from this very museum. The previous incident, which took place in 1998, was followed by the swift recovery of the paintings, both undamaged, and by the conviction and subsequent incarceration of the museum's then curator. But that's not all. Sisley's seemingly jinxed *Allé de Peupliers de Moret* had been lifted in yet another robbery, back in 1978, from a gallery in Marseille, where it happened to be on loan. Once again, it was found shortly afterwards, this time hidden in the sewers of Marseille. Unbelievable, perhaps. But true.

It is scarcely any wonder, then, that at the time of writing (when none of the paintings has yet reappeared) the art world is alight with speculation. Is some Bond villain archetype glorying over the stolen Sisley at his remote island lair? The evidence seems overwhelming that the paintings were stolen to order (experts agree that they are far too well known to be sold on the open market). The only question that remains is: whodunit?

good example the very beautiful 15th-century Flemish pictà. One for the specialists, perhaps, although the trip in itself is worth the effort, if only to get out of the centre and to catch a glimpse of one of the city's quieter, leafier residential neighbourhoods.

Villa Arson
20 avenue Stephen Liegeard (04 92 07 73 73/www.villa-arson.org). **Open** 10am-6pm Mon-Thur; 8.30am-4pm Sat. **Admission** free.
Set in vast parkland, this 18th-century villa is now under the aegis of the French cultural ministry as a catch-all centre for contemporary art. There's an art school on site, as well as the Centre National d'Art Contemporain, an exhibition space devoted to cutting-edge work grouped under certain themes. The recent 'Transmission' show, for instance, explored the use of various forms of communication in art, and included some exhibits by Turner Prize-winner Jeremy Deller. You can listen to heated discussions in the small café (8.30am-5pm Mon-Thur; 8.30am-3pm Fri) while you relax with a coffee.

Eating & drinking

L'Auberge de Théo
52 avenue Cap de Croix (04 93 81 26 19/www.auberge-de-theo.com). **Open** noon-2pm, 7-10.15pm Tue-Sat; noon-2pm Sun. Closed mid June-mid July. **€€**. **Italian**.
Head for the hills to taste some of Théo's fine Italian fare, or work in a lunch here between visits to the Cimiez museums. Expect to find a pleasant patio, plenty of top-notch grub (try the creamy escalope Valdostana) and friendly, attentive service.

Coco Beach
6 avenue Jean Lorrain (04 93 89 39 26/ www.cocobeach.fr). **Open** noon-1.45pm, 7.30-10pm Tue-Sat. **€€€**. **Seafood**.
It's an often-told but still charming story: on the site of this legendary restaurant, Jean-Baptiste Coco (a colourful local importer of wine and, among other things, sea sponges) made his

home in the 1930s, and became famous for the simple meals of grilled fish and rosé with which he would greet friends and visitors. These days, the restaurant bears only the name of M Coco, but endeavours to retain some of his Pagnolesque charm. The menu is a seafood feast, with the day's catch sold by the 100g and grilled with a minimum of fuss and a maximum of flavour. The terrace has a charming beach cabin aesthetic and perches right on the edge of the water offering views of the Baie des Anges that are ridiculously beautiful.

Liber Thé
46 boulevard Carlone (04 92 09 93 79). **Open** 8.30am-7.30pm Mon-Fri; 10am-4pm Sat. **€**. **Café**. No credit cards.
It's heartening to know that there are people like this around, working tirelessly in their local communities to create enthusiastic, fun and broad-minded cultural centres. First and foremost a bookshop, Liber Thé also has a small *salon de thé* operation at the front. Sit down, drink a brew and munch on a slice of cake while leafing through any of the volumes or periodicals that are scattered around (if you haven't finished what you're reading they may even let you borrow it). There's often a jazz pianist tinkling away in the background, as well as a regular programme of afternoon and evening events that encompasses everything from graffiti demonstrations through to musical recitals, children's theatre, modern dance and academic lectures on a wide variety of subjects. Small-scale art exhibitions (photos, mainly) are also a regular feature.

Nightlife

Blue Boy
9 rue Jean Baptiste Spinetta (04 93 44 68 24/www.blueboy.fr). **Open** 11.30pm-5am daily.
House music, pretty boys bearing their buff torsos and the guarantee of an up-for-it crowd make Blue Boy the most popular gay club in Nice. And if you like to dance in a mountain of soap

suds while wearing nothing but swimming trunks, you'll be right at home here on a Wednesday night.

Arts & leisure

Palais des Sports Jean Bouin

2 rue Jean Allègre (04 97 20 20 30). **Open** *Pool* 12.30-2pm Mon; 4-9pm Tue, Thur; 11am-5pm, 9-11pm Wed; 12.30-2pm, 9-11pm Fri; 10am-6pm Sat; 9am-6pm Sun. *Ice rink* 2-5.30pm Wed; 9pm-midnight Fri; 2-6pm, 10pm-1am Sat; 10-11.30am, 2-6pm Sun.

The main attractions of this vast sports complex are its Olympic-sized swimming pool and its impressive ice rink. The pool is clean and the rink is great fun (not to mention good value) if you're looking to have a change of scene (and climate). It also works well as a tool for appeasing children who've been dragged around one museum too many.

Palais Nikaïa

163 route de Grenoble (04 92 29 31 29/www.nikaia.fr). **Open** *Box office* 1-6pm Mon-Fri.

An 'amphitheatre of the modern world' is how this vast venue describes itself, although the action that takes place within the walls of its (52,000 capacity) outdoor stadium tends to be more musical than gladiatorial. Everyone from the late Pavarotti to U2 has played here at one time or another. But don't be surprised to find that Vanessa Paradis or Zucchero have been booked to play for the weekend that you're in town. It's nothing if not a mixed bag.

Théâtre Lino Ventura

168 boulevard de l'Ariane (04 97 00 10 70/www.tlv-nice.org). **Open** for performances.

It's a long journey northwards to this 700-seat auditorium (it's the city's second largest concert venue) but the calibre of the performers who choose to play here usually makes the trip more than worth the effort. The programme tends to favour a youth market, with recent bookings including Marseille's reggae superstars Massilia Sound System, and the underground hero of the French rap scene, La Fouine.

Musée Matisse p108

Cannes

'This, right here,' Henri taps the zinc bar top of his neighbourhood café emphatically, 'this is the real Cannes.' General murmurs of agreement come from the handful of other locals who are sipping their morning coffees, some of them nursing a small brandy on the side. Like Henri, they can remember this town when it was still scarcely more than a fishing village. He gestures in the direction of the far-off Croisette, his expression more one of resignation than resentment: 'That? That is Disneyland.'

When visiting Cannes, many tourists see little further than the seductive strip of luxury boutiques and palace hotels on the **Croisette** or the thriving eating, shopping and drinking hub of rue d'Antibes. The beaches that hug the Croisette are similarly showy, with some of the most expensive sun loungers on the coast, not to mention the hype and hip surrounding the annual film festival. But what of the rest of the town? The 'real Cannes'?

In terms of history, you'll find it all around you. Not so much in the museums and churches, of which there are far fewer than in Nice, but in the life of the street markets, and the cafés and bars that are set back a little from the shoreline. Towards **Le Suquet**, Cannes' oldest neighbourhood, is where much of its true character is still to be found. Again, the out-of-towners are targeted along the more picture-postcard streets (notably the cobbled **rue Saint Antoine**, with its myriad tourist restaurants and souvenir shops). But a few paces away, around the Forville

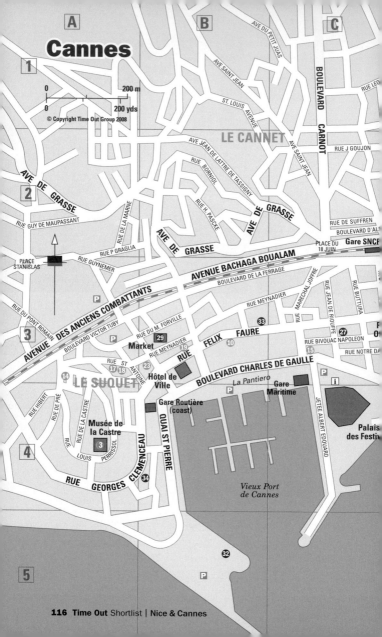

Cannes

A
B
C
1

AVE DU PETIT JUAS

AVE SAINT JEAN

BOULEVARD CARNOT

RUE LEO

0   200 m
0   200 yds
© Copyright Time Out Group 2008

ST. LOUIS AVENUE

ST. LOUIS

LE CANNET

RUE J GOUJON

2

AVE DE GRASSE

AVE JEAN DE LATTRE DE TASSIGNY

RUE BORRIOL

RUE H PASKE

RUE DE LA MARNE

AVE DE GRASSE

AVE DE GRASSE

RUE DE SUFFREN

BOULEVARD D'AL

RUE GUY DE MAUPASSANT

RUE P GRAGLIA

PLACE DU 18 JUIN

Gare SNCF

RUE GUYNEMER

AVENUE BACHAGA BOUALAM

PLACE STANISLAS

BOULEVARD DE LA FERRAGE

RUE DU PONT ROMAIN

RUE MEYNADIER

RUE MARÉCHAL JOFFRE

RUE JEAN DE RIOUFFE

RUE BUTTURA

3

AVENUE DES ANCIENS COMBATTANTS

BOULEVARD VICTOR TUBY

RUE DU M. FORVILLE

Market

33

RUE MEYNADIER

29

FELIX   FAURE

RUE BIVOUAC NAPOLEON

27

RUE NOTRE DA

RUE   ST   ANTOINE

19

RUE

10

15

RUE ST PRÉ

17 18

23

Hôtel de Ville

BOULEVARD CHARLES DE GAULLE

P

i

14

LE SUQUET

La Pantiero

Gare Maritime

RUE HIBERT

Gare Routière (coast)

P

4

RUE DE LA CASTRE

Musée de la Castre

3

RUE LOUIS PERRISSOL

QUAI ST PIERRE

Vieux Port de Cannes

JETÉE ALBERT EDOUARD

Palais des Festi

RUE   GEORGES   CLEMENCEAU

34

32

P

5

P

Market and at the top of the town, in the vicinity of the place du Suquet, there are still some gems to be discovered. Turn off the main roads to wander through the backstreets and you'll be rewarded.

Sights & museums

Espace Miramar

Corner rue Pasteur and boulevard de la Croisette (no phone). **Open** *June-Sept* 2-7pm Tue-Sun. *Oct-May* 1-6pm Tue-Sun. **Admission** free. **Map** p117 F4 ❶
It's worth checking to see which free exhibitions are on at this municipal gallery (photography is the most common medium to feature). There's also a small theatre and cinema, with an interesting programme of regular performances and projections.

La Malmaison

47 boulevard de la Croisette (04 97 06 44 90). **Open** *July-mid Sept* 11am-8pm Tue-Sun. *Mid Sept-June* 10am-1pm, 2.30-6.30pm Tue-Sun. **Admission** €3. **Map** p117 E4 ❷

The sole remnant of one of the Riviera's swankiest hotels (the Grand, which was almost entirely demolished in the 1960s), this attractive modern art museum now occupies what were once the hotel's tearoom and gaming rooms. Normally hosting at least three major exhibitions a year, Malmaison's intimate rooms have been graced by the works of such Côte d'Azur luminaries as Picasso, Ozenfant and Matisse. Robert Combas' recently commissioned fresco, *La Malmaison*, pays tribute to the city's enduring fascination with cinema.

Musée de la Castre

Le Suquet (04 93 38 55 26). **Open** *Apr-May, Sept* 10am-1pm, 2-6pm Tue-Sun. *June-Aug* 10am-1pm, 3-7pm Tue-Sun. *Oct-Mar* 10am-1pm, 2-5pm Tue-Sun. **Admission** €3. **Map** p116 A4 ❸
The picturesque hilltop location (in the ruins of a medieval castle) certainly plays a part in the charm of this eccentric yet fascinating museum. In many ways, the permanent exhibition is of

Le Carlton p121

niche interest, a kind of homage to the Victorian mania for collecting and cataloguing anthropological data. The main collection consists of the arcane legacy of Baron Lycklama, an intrepid and widely travelled Dutch aristocrat. The trappings of Lycklama's travels, and those of fellow 19th-century adventurer and journalist Ginoux de la Coche, comprise a hotchpotch of ethnic artefacts, weaponry and ceramics, garnered from territories as diverse as the Himalayas and Polynesia. Interspersed with these are various other objects of archaeological and ethnological interest from the less far-flung shores of the Mediterranean. Provençal and local paintings from 19th- and 20th-century artists occupy a further three rooms, and there is a sizeable collection of some 200 musical instruments from Asia, Africa and Central America. Also included in the ticket price is access to the 12th-century tower that rises up from the museum's courtyard, and from whose summit the views of Cannes and its bay are nothing short of spectacular.

Eating & drinking

With the major ongoing works at the Majestic Barrière hotel, one of the most prestigious fine-dining restaurants in Cannes has been temporarily displaced: the **Villa de Lys** was, at the time of writing, seeking new premises until work on the hotel has been completed. Contact the Majestic Barrière (p147) for further information.

38 The Restaurant

Hôtel Gray d'Albion, 38 rue des Serbes (04 92 99 79 60/www.gray-dalbion.com). **Open** 12.30-2pm, 7.30-10pm Tue-Sat. €€. **Global.** **Map** p117 D3 ④

A menu offering a sophisticated take on 'world cuisine' matches the contemporary dark wood furniture and coffee-coloured upholstery of the sexily curved banquettes at this high-end hotel diner. Favoured by business-lunchers and smart, fashionable locals, 38 also has a decent wine list and a troupe of attentive, professional staff.

Le 72 Croisette

72 boulevard de la Croisette (04 93 94 18 30). **Open** *May-Oct* 7am-4am daily. *Nov-Apr* 7am-9pm daily. **Bar**. Map p117 F5 ❺

Not as heavily made-up as the other bars on the strip, the 72 is refreshingly unpretentious, especially given its location opposite the iconic Martinez hotel. Elbow your way to a seat with a view of the hotel's forecourt, where the arrival of stretched, tinted and otherwise customised luxury vehicles makes for great people-watching. Remember: the big ones with the suits that look like they've shrunk in the wash are the bodyguards, the ones wearing the Police shades are the big shots.

L'Affable

5 rue Lafontaine (04 93 68 02 09/ www.restaurant-laffable.fr). **Open** noon-2pm, 7-10.30pm Mon-Fri; 7-10.30pm Sat. **€€**. **French**. Map p117 E3 ❻

Smartly upholstered leather banquettes and discreet decor give the dining room here a certain cachet, although it's the cooking that really steals the show. Pan-seared tuna with shallot reduction or tender veal with morels are examples from a modestly ambitious menu. Decent wines, too.

Al Charq Spécialités Libanaises

20 rue Rouaze (04 93 94 01 76/ www.alcharq.com). **Open** 11am-11pm Tue-Sun. **€€**. **Middle Eastern**. Map p117 F4 ❼

Restaurant, café and *traiteur* rolled into one, this busy and dependable Lebanese-run establishment continues to serve some of the best falafel in town. It's a great place to rest your legs over lunch (it's tucked just off the tourist trail, behind the Martinez) or to stock up for some picnic provisions of your own.

L'Alhambra

1 rue du Ratéguier (04 93 38 96 11). **Open** 5pm-midnight Mon, Wed-Sun. **€€**. **French**. Map p117 E3 ❽

Former Paris Saint-Germain and Nice footballer José Cobos is the owner of this slick new restaurant just off the Croisette. The traditional provençal dishes are given the occasional Spanish spin, but the more straightforward offerings (such as *souris d'agneau*) are also worth a punt.

Amiral Bar

Le Martinez, 73 La Croisette (04 92 98 73 00/www.hotel-martinez.com). **Open** 11am-2.30am daily. **Bar**. Map p117 F5 ❾

A serious bar, this one: the barmen are award-winning mixologists, the pianist has played Carnegie Hall, and the customers are dressed head to toe in designer threads. Take a seat, sip an Old Fashioned and make eye contact with a beautiful stranger. Drinks don't come cheap, but it's worth paying a little extra to feel like Cary Grant for a few minutes.

Astoux et Brun

27 rue Félix Faure (04 93 39 21 87). **Open** noon-3.30pm, 7-11.30pm daily. **€€**. **Seafood**. Map p116 B3 ❿

You may be sitting on white plastic furniture, with not a great deal of elbow room in between you and your fellow diners, but what a visit to this long-established restaurant does guarantee is that you will be eating the best seafood in Cannes. The *plateaux de fruits de mer* are colourful, glistening still lives of abundance; the freshly shucked oysters are rock pools of intense minerally flavour. Crisp white wines, good, brisk service and the occasional reports of hefty claw-crackers complete the picture.

Bar des Célébrités

Le Carlton, 58 boulevard de la Croisette (04 93 06 40 06/www.ichotelsgroup. com). **Open** 11am-1am daily. **Bar**. Map p117 F4 ⓫

Don't worry, they will still let you in if you're not a celebrity. Although it must be said that, wandering out on to the bar's sea-facing terrace, with live jazz filling the evening air, it can be quite easy to suddenly feel that you are, in fact, famous. If only for the 15 minutes it takes to drink a cocktail.

NICE & CANNES BY AREA

La Brouette de Grandmère

9 bis rue d'Oran (04 93 39 12 10).
Open 7.30-11pm daily. **€€. French.**
Map p117 F3 ⑫

Literally meaning 'grandmother's wheelbarrow', this popular and convivial little restaurant serves a brand of traditional cuisine that many French people might associate with nostalgic memories of their granny's cooking. But not quite so many will get the same twinge of remembrance about the shot of vodka or glass of champagne that are presented during the course of the meal. But who cares? It's great fun, and great value, thanks to the 'one menu, one price' formula.

Café Lenôtre

63 rue d'Antibes (04 97 06 67 67/ www.lenotre.fr). **Open** 9am-7pm Mon-Sat. **€€. Café. Map** p117 D3 ⑬

With franchises as far afield as Osaka and Dubai, this chain of café-épiceries has apparently hit on a magic formula for worldwide appeal to the masses. And yet despite – or it because of this – the quality remains commendably high. The 'boutique' operation on the ground floor of this branch tempts high-street shoppers with a wide range of the signature pastries, artisanal chocolates and various tasty savoury snacks. But the main business is the café, either upstairs or on the sunny terrace, where breakfast, lunch and tea menus tout the goodies on display in the shop, plus a wide variety of imaginatively cooked dishes. There's also a small cookery school on the premises, offering laidback lessons for adults and children alike.

Café Los Faroles

1 rue Pré (04 93 39 20 32). **Open** 9am-9pm Mon-Sat. **€€. Brasserie. Map** p116 A3 ⑭

During the morning, this unpretentious little bar/restaurant serves coffees, drinks and snacks to the various locals and tourists who are either about to go down or have just climbed up rue Saint Antoine. Come lunch, or early evening, and the chef fires up the stove in the small exposed kitchen before trotting out a selection of tasty plats du jour – omelette, steak, fish of the day, and so on. Friendly service and quaffable wines increase the already considerable feel-good factor.

Café Roma

1 square Mérimée (04 93 38 05 04). **Open** *Sept-June* 7.30am-2.30am daily. *July, Aug* 7.30am-4am daily. **€. Café. Map** p116 C3 ⑮

True to its name, this perennially busy café serves decent coffee and some more than passable pasta dishes. Given its location on the busy square opposite the Palais des Festivals, it's either a poseur's paradise or prime territory for people-watching, depending on your predilections.

Cannelle

Hôtel Gray d'Albion, 32 rue des Serbes (04 93 38 72 79). **Open** 9am-5pm Mon-Sat. **€€. Café/Traiteur. Map** p117 D3 ⑯

It's hard not to work up a wolfish appetite among the cornucopia of fine foods on offer at this upmarket café-cum-grocer. Buy to take away or hope you're lucky enough to bag a seat at one of the handful of tables for a light bite (quiche, pasata and whatnot, all done to a high standard).

Le Mantel

22 rue Saint Antoine (04 93 39 13 10). **Open** noon-2pm Mon, Tue, Fri-Sun. **€€€. Haute cuisine. Map** p116 A3 ⑰

The eponymous Noël Mantel has a reputation and clientele that extends far beyond Cannes' city limits. The crisp white tablecloths and artisanal breads that adorn the tables of his straightforwardly stylish restaurant look a little out of place on the often rather tacky rue Saint Antoine. Yet that doesn't seem to deter the hordes of locals and gastronomically minded tourists who keep the place busy year-round. It is necessary to book ahead if you want to sample the highly accomplished seasonal French fare.

Le Mesclun

16 rue Saint Antoine (04 93 99 45 19/ www.lemesclun-restaurant.com). **Open** 7-11pm Mon-Sat. **€€**. **French**. Map p116 A3 ⑱

Wood panelling, elegant table settings, a wine rack laden with well-chosen bottles: it is apparent from the outset that this is a restaurant with serious intentions. And the kitchen's modish takes on traditional southern cuisine are proof that the same attention to detail applies behind the scenes as well. Roasted sea bass with artichoke marmalade or parsley-crusted rack of lamb are typical of the dishes served.

O'tchan

4 rue Félix Faure (04 93 39 16 37). **Open** 8.30am-7pm Mon-Sat. **€€**. **Bar/Café**. Map p116 B3 ⑲

This is definitely somewhere to come on those days when you wish your body felt more like a temple and less like a Bermondsey lock-up. Water is the main system-purifier (there are a dozen or so to choose from, including Vass from Norway or good old English Hildon), with a long list of herbal and fruit teas also on hand to flush away the toxins. A plat du jour is offered at lunch – roasted cod with saffron rice last time we stopped by – along with a few snacks to fill the gaps.

Le Palme d'Or

Le Martinez, 73 La Croisette (04 92 98 73 00/www.hotel-martinez.com). **Open** 12.30-2pm, 8-10pm Tue-Sat. **€€€€**. **Haute cuisine**. Map p117 F5 ⑳

One of the finest restaurants in town, this sophisticated hotel diner has established a cast-iron reputation in recent years, thanks in no small part to the culinary talents of chef Christian Sinicropi. Having recently inherited the top toque from departing maestro Christian Willer, Sinicropi has been pleasing palates with dishes like turbot roasted with fennel and mango, or roast duck served with stuffed pear and a chocolate-infused sauce. A seriously good nosebag, then, but with the serious prices to match: a main course

can set you back as much as €135, and that's before you've even had time to look through the wine list.

Pause Café

39 rue Hoche (04 93 39 83 03). **Open** 9am-7.30pm Mon-Sat. **€€**. **Café**. Map p117 D3 ㉑

A decent little brasserie, the Pause is an ideal pit stop if you find yourself at this end of the shopping strip come lunchtime. They rustle up a mean steak tartare, among other things, and the coffee is excellent.

Le Restaurant Arménien

82 boulevard de la Croisette (04 93 94 00 58/www.lerestaurantarmenien.com). **Open** *July, Aug* 7-10.30pm daily. *Sept-June* 7-10.30pm Tue-Sat; noon-2.30pm, 7-10.30pm Sun. **€€**. **Armenian**. Map p117 F4 ㉒

Now here's a real one-off for Riviera dining: an Armenian restaurant with a fine culinary pedigree and loyal fans. Vegetarians adore the delicate meze dishes, die-hard carnivores demolish the kebabs, and the gastronomically curious revel in the regional specialities (not to mention the idiosyncratic menu translations: 'salad of believed cabbage heart', anyone?). In short, delicious food, warm service and a stonking wine list make this as close as you can get to a guaranteed good night out.

La Taverne Lucullus

4 place Marché Forville (04 93 39 32 74). **Open** 5am-3pm Tue-Sun. **Bar**. No credit cards. **Map** p116 B3 ㉓

Within earshot of the brash, demotic chorus of the city's colourful food market, this low-key locals' bar opens in time to fortify the stall-holders before the day's work begins. And it closes shortly after it has finished catering to the outgoing shoppers (most of whom are friends, acquaintances, regulars or just plain lost). A daily dish is rustled up at lunch from the spoils of the day's market visit, and lively conversation (only start one about football if you really know what you're talking about), decent coffee and cold beer are on the menu all day. As authentic as it gets.

La Terrasse

148 boulevard de la République (04 93 68 40 83/www.oxfordhotel.fr). **Open** *May-Sept* noon-2pm, 7-10pm Mon-Sat. *Oct-Apr* noon-2pm Mon-Sat. €€. **French**. Map p117 D1 ㉔

You'll work up an appetite on the walk to this north-of-centre hotel restaurant, but an enthusiastic welcome and an interesting, affordable menu are the prizes when you make it to the other end. Seasonal provençal dishes jostle for menu space with spicier, more globally influenced fare, while the concise wine list keeps it strictly local. The eponymous terrace looks out on the abundant greenery of the hotel's garden. A relaxing place to eat.

Les Vincennes

83 avenue de Lérins (04 93 43 15 66). **Open** noon-2.30pm, 7-10.30pm Mon, Tue, Thur-Sat; noon-2.30pm Sun. €€. **French**. Map p117 F4 ㉕

Carnivores are welcomed with open arms at this family restaurant where tartare is the house speciality. The tartare au cognac, prepared table-side, is particularly recommended.

Volupté

41 rue Hoche (04 93 39 60 32/ www.volupte-cannes.com). **Open** 9am-7.30pm Mon-Sat. €. **Café**. Map p117 D3 ㉖

Looking a little like a lounge in a boutique hotel, this gourmet café has an amazing selection of teas from around the world. Everything from first-flush Darjeeling through to Angel's Kiss green tea is on the menu, along with a handful of snack-sized gap-fillers, of the cake, pastry and pudding varieties. If you want to carry on doing this kind of thing at home, you can wander a few doors down to no.32 and pick up some tea from the shop.

Shopping

Scratch-card winners, wealthy residents and blue-chip tourists tend to confine their shopping activities to the parallel pleasures of the Croisette and rue d'Antibes.

The former has pretty much every luxury clothing, jewellery and fashion boutique going. To name but a few of the many well-known names present and correct: Chanel (no.5); Fendi (no.44); Bulgari (no.19); Hermès (no.17); Christian Dior (no.38); Louis Vuitton (no.22); Cartier (no.57). Rue d'Antibes has its fair share of high-end stores too, as well as a few more affordable options, such as Mango (no.84).

But the real heart of Cannes is a long way from the boutique bling of the new town. You'll need to head further west to get a flavour of where and how the cannois do their shopping. The pedestrianised rue Meynadier has many budget clothing and fashion stores, but you'll also find lots of traditional food and wine stores, as well as delicatessens selling all manner of local and foreign produce, at affordable prices. Just a few steps north of here is the wonderful Forville Market.

Cannes English Bookshop

11 rue Bivouac Napoléon (04 93 99 40 08). **Open** 10am-6.45pm Mon-Sat. Map p116 C3 ㉗

Testament to the fact that the region's Anglophone population is as robust (and literary minded) as ever, this charming bookshop continues to thrive after nearly a quarter of a century in business. Thousands of titles are stocked, ranging from the arcane to the airport thriller, and it's not unheard of for regional writers to come and scribble their names in a few copies, either – Peter Mayle being a recent example.

FNAC

83 rue d'Antibes (04 97 06 29 29/ www.fnac.com). **Open** 10am-7pm Mon-Sat. Map p117 E3 ㉘

As with the other links in France's formidable one-stop culture shop, this branch of FNAC has every possible book, movie, CD and electronic gizmo to keep boredom at arm's length.

Le Suquet p115

Forville Market

rue Forville (no phone). **Open** 6am-1pm daily. **Map** p116 B3 ㉙
Other than Mondays, when there's a weekly flea market, this historic covered market is alive with that special blend of haggling, browsing, sniffing and squeezing that is the unique preserve of French food markets. And yet, unlike some of the more touristy affairs dotted around the south, this is the real deal. Gutsy, loud, busy (get those elbows out) and commendably good value, Forville has a massive range of excellent farm produce, seafood, dairy goods, fruit and so much more. Stallholders truck in from miles around to offload the cream of their crops, and everyone from shuffling grannies to office juniors comes here to shop in the time-honoured fashion: one day at a time.

Nightlife

Le Loft

13 rue du Docteur Monod (06 13 83 10 24/www.dalton-group.com). **Open** 9pm-2.30am Wed-Sat. **Map** p117 E4 ㉚
The city's main clubbing spot, the Loft stirs things up with a mainstream mix of hip hop, house and electro. The DJs here aren't looking to get the trainspotter seal of approval on their playlists, they're just aiming to bring the dancefloor up to warp speed by midnight. Which they invariably succeed in doing. You may want to indulge in a bit of concept dining in the Tantra restaurant downstairs (or, better still, elsewhere) before heading up for a post-prandial shimmy, as the club itself can be a bit on the slow side until the second half of the evening.

Morrison Lounge

10 rue Teisseire (04 92 98 16 17/ www.morrisonspub.com). **Open** 5pm-2am Mon-Fri; 1pm-2am Sat, Sun. **Map** p117 E3 ㉛
One part Irish pub, one part lounge-style club, Morrison's is a raucous cocktail of drinking and dancing. It's generally a good laugh (as long as you've not come here in search of a quiet night) and, somewhat predictably, it's utter mayhem on St Patrick's Day. Also, if you're not sure how to read a map, the owners have thoughtfully posted a YouTube video link on their website, which gives step-by-step instructions on how to get here.

Arts & leisure

Boat tours

Ile Saint Honorat: Planaria, quai Laubeuf (04 92 98 71 38). Ile Sainte Marguerite: Trans Côte d'Azur, quai Laubeuf (04 92 98 71 30). **Open** *Both* 7.30am-5pm daily. **Map** p116 B5 ㉜
Boats depart every hour to each of the Iles de Lérins, although neither of the companies offers a service to both destinations. Planaria, the ferry company that services Ile Saint Honorat, is privately owned by the monks who live there. Trans Côte d'Azur operates the vedette to Ile Sainte Marguerite. Both companies charge €11 for an adult return and, in both cases, the journey lasts no longer than 15 minutes.

Cinéma Les Arcades

77 rue Félix Faure (04 93 39 00 98). **Open** According to programme. **Map** p116 B3 ㉝
Admittedly, it's not quite the same thing as the film festival, but this *version originale* (English-language) cinema shows a decent programme of Hollywood and Brit-flick new releases. Customers tend to be a mix of local expats getting a fix of memories from home, and tourists who can either think of nothing better to do or who need the darkness and comfort of a cinema to salve stubborn hangovers.

SYLPA Plongée

10 rue de la Rampe (04 93 38 67 57/ www.plongee-sylpa.com). **Open** *Apr-Dec* According to schedule. Closed Jan-Mar. **Map** p116 B4 ㉞
The life aquatic is the speciality here, with diving and snorkelling outings offered to all abilities and ages. The rendezvous point is on quai Saint Pierre in the Vieux Port – look out for

Ile Saint Honorat

the boat with the 'SYLPA' logo. Groups are catered for, as are those wishing to pursue a PADI certificate, but the bulk of visitors are gunning for the half-day (€45) 'Baptême' introductory session.

Ile Saint Honorat

Part of what makes this tiny island community of Cistercian monks seem so beguiling to the casual visitor is the proximity of their wild and beautiful territory to the unreal, sanitised glamour of Cannes, just a couple of kilometres across the water.

Unlike its nearest neighbour (Ile Sainte Marguerite), Ile Saint Honorat requires visitors to observe certain rules and to respect the traditions of the life there (no loud noises, no inappropriate clothing, and so on). Home to a small community of around 25 Cistercian monks, the island's life continues as it has for centuries, and the hope is that tourism will do little to disrupt this momentum, and much to finance it. Those who are curious to know more about the life of the monks are welcome to attend morning masses during the week (at 11.25am) and on Sunday (at 9.50am) in the Eglise Abbatiale de Lérins. There is even a selective programme of silent retreats extended to (male) visitors who can satisfactorily convince the abbot that they have a significant spiritual interest in the brotherhood and wish to spend some time within its cloisters.

Most of us, however, only want to remain for a day, which in fact is about all the time you'll need to really get to grips with the natural and historic assets of the island. It's possible to make it around the coastline in a matter of a few hours, but it takes a little longer to get the real flavour of the place.

When exploring the vicinity of the 19th-century monastery (where the cloisters are, and where today's monks live, work and pray), you'll get glimpses of the life that continues here after the tour boats have left. Discreet banks of solar panels lighten the load on the monastic coffers, while more than seven hectares of vineyards supply the island's boutique wine-making industry. Then, just a short walk around the coastal path, the historic **Monastère Fortifié** catapults you right back through the centuries, offering an insight into the inception (and tenacity) of this insular and erudite community.

Sights & musuems

Monastère Fortifié

Ile St Honorat (04 92 99 54 00/ www.abbayedelerins.com). **Open** 10am-4.30pm daily. **Admission** *Oct-June* free. *July-Sept* €2. No credit cards Construction began in the 11th century, and for the next 300 years, this medieval keep's fortifications were gradually augmented as the monks strove to withstand attacks from pirates and sundry would-be invaders from across the Mediterranean. Those doughty monks sustained their existence in much the same way as their contemporary counterparts, as evidenced by the bread oven and olive press discovered in the basement here. The additional levels of the monastery were devoted, in ascending order, to prayer and military activities.

Eating & drinking

La Tonelle

Ile St Honorat (04 92 99 18 07). **Open** *Apr-Oct* 9am-5pm daily. Closed Nov-Mar. **€. Snack.** Just the type of restaurant you'd expect to find on an island that is inhabited by monks, La Tonelle is a simple sort of self-service operation with tasty sarnies, salads and wraps, good coffee and ecologically minded wooden cutlery and paper plates.

Ile Sainte Marguerite

Heavily forested, redolent of warm pine needles and salt air, and skirted by white-sand beaches, Ile Sainte Marguerite is just the right size to explore in a leisurely day of strolling, picnicking and swimming.

The largest of the two Iles de Lérins (the two diminutive islands that sit a couple of kilometres offshore in the Rade de Cannes), Sainte Marguerite is a manageable three kilometres (two miles) long by one kilometre (just over half a mile) wide. A maze of small sentiers (forest paths) wind off through copses of pine and eucalyptus, emerging at secluded beaches and calanques, where warm water and the absence of any offshore currents or rips make for ideal bathing and snorkelling conditions. A high traffic of day trippers in summer means you'll be sharing your little corner of azure Med with any number of others but the crowds here tend to be far less brash and showy than those who sun themselves on the beaches that hug the Croisette in Cannes proper.

Various ruins and historical sites are dotted around the place, but it's only really worth rolling up your sun mat to make the trip to **Fort Royal** and, once inside, to the **Musée de la Mer** (the highlight of which is the cell in which the mysterious Man in the Iron Mask was held captive during the reign of Louis XIV). That said, during the high season, some young and highly enthusiastic representatives of Cannes Tourist Office have a couple of small stalls set up (one at the disembarkation point of the ferry, one up near the fort) to point visitors in the right direction. Find out from them if they are operating any guided walks – it's well worth tagging along if you want to find out more about the Ligurian and Roman ruins dotted around, and the history of the island as a fortified military outpost.

Sights & musuems

Fort Royal

Ile Ste Marguerite (04 93 38 55 26). **Open** *June-Sept* 10am-5.45pm daily. *Oct-Mar* 10.30am-1.15pm, 2.15-4.45pm Tue-Sun. *Apr, May* 10.30am-1.15pm, 2.15-5.45pm Tue-Sun. **Admission** €3.
Begun by the Spanish during their occupation of the island in the Thirty Years War, construction of the Fort Royal was finished off by the French (under the auspices of the great military architect Vauban) in the second half of the 17th century. These days, the former stronghold and prison serves as an educational and training centre, as well as a much-visited historical landmark.

Musée de la Mer

Fort Royal, Ile Ste Marguerite (04 93 38 55 26). **Open** *June-Sept* 10am-5.45pm daily. *Oct-Mar* 10.30am-1.15pm, 2.15-4.45pm Tue-Sun. *Apr, May* 10.30am-1.15pm, 2.15-5.45pm Tue-Sun. **Admission** €3.
Most famous for containing the jail cell once occupied by the Man in the Iron Mask, this former prison block is now a catch-all museum exhibiting the quarters, artefacts and correspondence of its erstwhile inmates. Also among the displays are some Roman remains discovered in nearby excavations, as well as the cargo from two shipwrecks (one also dating from the Roman era, the other from the tenth century).

Eating & drinking

La Guérite

Near Fort Royal (04 93 43 49 30). **Open** *Apr-Sept* 11am-6pm daily. Closed Oct-Mar. **€€. French.**
At the foot of the hill beneath the Musée de la Mer, this beachside restaurant does a good line in fresh fish. The grilled langoustines and lobsters from the *viviers* are especially fresh, making the journey from life to plate in minutes.

Essentials

La Pérouse p135

Hotels

With France's busiest airport outside Paris shipping in tourists by the thousand, Nice's hotel industry has gone from good to through-the-roof in recent years. More than 10,000 hotel rooms are dotted around the city, and yet still it can be a struggle to get heads on beds during high season and festival time (Nice Jazz Festival and the Carnaval de Nice, in particular). Book in advance, then, to be sure of avoiding disappointment.

And disappointed is the last thing you will be if you decide to go stellar and check in to one of the palace hotels, like the **Negresco** in Nice or the **Martinez** in Cannes. However, some of the young pretenders are giving the old guard a run for their money with bleeding-edge design, digital-age facilities and trendier-than-thou

drinking and dining: foremost among this band of newcomers is the **Hi Hôtel** at the eastern edge of Nice's New Town, and **Hôtel 3.14**, keeping up the cool work down the coast in Cannes.

But the lifeblood of the Côte's hotel industry is its many smaller, family-run hotels that specialise in that particular brand of southern French hospitality – breakfast on the terrace, sunny guestrooms and enthusiastic staff, proud of their city and happy to take the time to point you in the direction of a relative's bar or a favourite stall at the market. Places like **Villa la Tour** (one of the rare hotels in Vieux Nice) or **Hôtel Molière**, squirreled away in the heart of Cannes, are typical examples. But you won't need to look long to find many, many more.

The chains, too, have a good presence up and down the coast, with Nice's **Four Points Sheraton Elysée Palace** being a particularly popular stop. And just to clear up any confusion: the most famous of the palace hotels, the Regina, where Queen Victoria and Matisse once stayed (although not – *quelle horreur* – together), may still exist as a building, and indeed may have retained its name, but it is no longer a hotel. It was converted as far back as the 1930s into an apartment block and is home to some of the city's wealthiest denizens. So don't go knocking.

Vieux Nice

Beau Rivage

24 rue Saint François de Paule (04 92 47 82 82/www.nicebeaurivage.com). €€€.
It would take quite a leap of the imagination to place this hotel's most famous former guest, Henri Matisse, among the sleek, architect-led design of its modern incarnation. Little from the artist's era remains after a comprehensive 2004 refurb launched Beau Rivage into the ranks of design accommodation, where it is now firmly rooted. A slightly Zen aesthetic (think artfully distributed piles of pebbles and plenty of natural light) permeates the public areas, while the similarly contemporary but somehow quite cosy rooms are characterised by neutral colour schemes, crisp bed linen, elegant shutters and porthole light fittings. The hotel has its own beach (with an attendant restaurant) but, being a few streets back from the prom, its views extend only as far as the old town's rooftops.

Hôtel Suisse

15 quai Rauba Capeu (04 92 17 39 00). €€.
A real bargain, and well worth making the effort of booking in advance, Hôtel Suisse is unlikely to disappoint. For one thing, it has wonderful views of the bay and the beaches from its position

SHORTLIST

Best for luxury
- Le Carlton (p144)
- Château de la Tour (p144)
- Le Martinez (p147)
- Le Negresco (p141)
- Le Palais de la Méditerranée (p141)
- La Pérouse (p135)

Best sea views
- Hotel Palais Maeterlinck (p143)
- Le Palais de la Méditerranée (p141)
- La Pérouse (p135)
- Sofitel Cannes Le Méditerranée (p149)

Best for design
- Le Cavendish (p144)
- Hi Hôtel (p136)
- Hôtel 3.14 (p144)
- Hôtel Ellington (p136)
- Le Windsor (p141)

Best bargain beds
- La Belle Meunière (p135)
- L'Excelsior (p135)
- Hôtel de la Buffa (p136)
- Hôtel de la Fontaine (p136)
- Hôtel du Petit Palais (p143)
- Villa la Tour (p135)
- Le Wilson (p139)

Best for taking a picturesque dip
- Château de la Tour (p144)
- Le Palais de la Méditerranée (p141)
- La Pérouse (p135)
- Le Splendid (p139)

Best for art lovers
- Le Negresco (p141)
- Le Wilson (p139)
- Le Windsor (p141)

Best breakfast
- Le Grimaldi (p136)
- Hôtel Oxford (p147)
- Le Splendid (p139)
- Villa La Tour (p135)

ESSENTIALS

Villa La Tour

ESSENTIALS

on quai Rauba Capeu (it's definitely worth splashing out a few extra euros in order to get a room with a sea view) and, what's more, the hotel itself is meticulously maintained. The helpful, easy-going staff, and a location that's close to town but far enough away to be peaceful, are added extras.

La Pérouse

11 quai Rauba Capeu (04 93 62 34 63/www.hotel-la-perouse.com). €€€.

The sunny yellow façade and lovely terracotta roof tiles of this seriously swanky hotel are picture-postcard perfect against the backdrop of the Colline du Château, from which vantage point the Pérouse commands peerless views of the bay and the sun-kissed spires of Vieux Nice. The sundeck, sauna and gorgeous infinity pool with sea views add to the sense of a hilltop eyrie, a vibe shared by the immaculate guestrooms and secluded dining areas, both inside and out. On the down side, though, some of the rooms are very small, and the staff can be snooty.

Villa La Tour

4 rue de la Tour (04 93 80 08 15/ www.villa-la-tour.com). €.

If you want to be right in the heart of the old-town action, there's simply nowhere better in Nice to stay. Set in a converted 18th-century convent, this idiosyncratic hotel has a loyal following, and it's easy to see why. The buffet breakfast is a lively affair, awash with good food and coffee, and some friendly chat between staff and guests. The individually decorated rooms, characterful hallways and sweet little roof terrace further reinforce the sense of being a guest in a quirky family house. And perhaps most important of all, it is excellent value, with some of the most affordable room rates in town.

New Town

La Belle Meunière

21 avenue Durante (04 93 88 66 15/ www.bellemeuniere.com). Closed Dec-Jan. €.

Intimate, affordable and really rather lovely, the Belle Meunière is one of those rare treats: a budget hotel with genuine charm. Were it not for the small blue plaque above the door announcing it as a hotel, it would be easy to mistake this pretty little house, just a few steps from the train station, for a private home. Rooms inside are clean and simply furnished but have plenty of character, while the small, tree-shaded garden is a popular hangout for the hotel's more youthful and transient clientele to kick back and trade backpacker stories.

Les Cigales

16 rue Dalpozzo (04 97 03 10 70/ www.hotel-lescigales.com). €€.

Guestrooms are comfortable and cheerfully decorated at this family-run former *hôtel particulier* in the heart of Nice. It's a convenient location but far enough from the hurly burly of Vieux Nice's bars and the main drag of the New Town to retain a sense of calm and the promise of an undisturbed night's sleep (rooms are also well soundproofed). Some of the rooms have small balconies overlooking the garden.

L'Excelsior

19 avenue Durante (04 93 88 18 05/ www.excelsiornice.com). €.

From its grand 1898 façade to the lush vegetation and towering palm of its tranquil garden, the Excelsior is every inch the old-school Riviera hotel. Not quite in the Woosterish league of the Negresco and others, it still retains a vestigial whiff of the Côte's golden age, and its clean, comfortable rooms set the mood with views of the cloistered interior courtyard or the quiet, typically niçois street out front.

Le Gounod

3 rue Gounod (04 93 16 42 00/ www.gounod-nice.com). Closed mid Nov-mid Dec. €€.

The creamy yellow façade and beautiful early-20th century porch of this smart hotel are the impressive old-world shell for what is otherwise a resolutely modern operation. Guestrooms are comfortable and perfectly pleasant, while those with balconies are quite charming. The Gounod also has an arrangement that allows its guests to make use of the rooftop pool at the four-star Le Splendid around the corner.

Le Grimaldi

15 rue Grimaldi (04 93 16 00 24/ www.le-grimaldi.com). €€€.
This is the kind of smart, townhouse hotel where you get the feeling that you are really being looked after. Staff know who you are, the rooms are tastefully furnished (in a subtly updated provençal style) and bountifully equipped with good-quality products, comfortable furnishings and fixtures. The superbly old-fashioned lift makes you feel like you're in a Simenon novel, and the views from the rooms on the rue Maccarani side, overlooking the diminutive Eglise Reformée de Nice, are similarly evocative. The lobby area makes for a pleasantly cool and relaxed environment to plan the day's excursions (with a computer room annex on hand for any last-minute Googling), and the complimentary breakfast buffet would satisfy even the most wolfish appetite.

Hi Hôtel

3 avenue des Fleurs (04 97 07 26 26/ www.hi-hotel.net). €€€.
Aficionados of boutique chic will stay nowhere else in Nice. The Hi Hôtel simply has it all, from hip, smart and functional public spaces to organic menus and a state-of-the-art hammam, while not forgetting, of course, some of the coolest accommodation on the Riviera. Rooms and suites seem to have been designed to correspond to the differing moods of the city. The funky 'techno' rooms, for example, provide the ideal recovery space for nighthawks and clubbers on tour, while the 'white & white' rooms cater to just the opposite market, offering serene and restful retreats for ethereal flâneurs. Whether it's a retro *Barbarella* vibe you want or a mini design temple with cast-iron lava bath, this place has it all. DJs provide a dance-music soundtrack on some nights, either on the panoramic roof terrace or down below, in the hotel's bar. There's also a small pool, a sweet interior courtyard and an abundance of helpful, switched-on staff.

Hôtel de la Buffa

56 rue de la Buffa (04 93 88 77 35/ www.hotel-buffa.com). €.
Amazingly good value, given its central location, the Buffa is what you'd call bog standard accommodation, but by no means devoid of charm for that. Warm and welcoming staff, and clean, cosy rooms more than make up for the absence of any design flourishes.

Hôtel de la Fontaine

49 rue de France (04 93 88 30 38/ www.hotel-fontaine.com). €.
Spruce, friendly and great value, the Fontaine is well worth checking into. Its charming inner courtyard, complete with *lavoir* and fragrant plants creeping up the walls, has the calm and secluded atmosphere of a provincial village square. Rooms, while nothing fancy, are smart and welcoming, and the breakfast buffet (included in the room rate) is enough to set you up for a day of energetic sightseeing.

Hôtel Ellington

25 boulevard Dubouchage (04 92 47 79 79/www.ellington-nice.com). €€€.
Opened in December 2006, this elegant, upmarket newcomer has already become one of the smartest addresses in town. Set right on the cusp of the New Town, on a boulevard of stately apartment buildings, the Ellington is an opulent operation, with all the mod cons tucked discreetly away behind its retro aesthetic. Chandeliers, period lamps and beautiful leather armchairs give the lobby and lounge the glamorous feel of a previous era (you find yourself half expecting to see Audrey Hepburn swish past), while the rooms themselves live comfortably in the era of flat-screen television and comfort-led ergonomic design. The bar makes a pleasant setting for a bracer before heading out for the evening, or a quick snort after getting back.

Palatial awareness

Always rooms to improve at the Negresco.

There is no elixir of eternal youth in the hotel game; the secret to staying one ahead is learning how to grow old gracefully. That, at least, seems to be the philosophy that keeps Nice's most famous palace hotel, the **Negresco** (p141), a step ahead of the competition. There is always something new happening here. Not in the hip kind of way that keeps the doors of its boutique rivals opening – let's face it, you won't be seeing this hotel's stately bar on any DJ flyers – but a nip here, a tuck there. Just enough to keep its dignity (and blue-chip guest list) intact.

The latest change, however, has been a big one, bringing a transfusion of young blood into the hotel's kitchens. Award-winning thirtysomething Jean-Denis Rieubland has replaced Bruno Turbot (now departed after two decades) at the command post of the Negresco's famous Chantecler restaurant, clutching a CV that reads like a *Who's Who* of culinary France. What impact this

will have remains to be seen, but the early signs are promising. Rieubland's insistence on high quality local produce, and his intricate elaborations of regional dishes, are unlikely to alienate the existing troupe of regulars and may even recruit some new ones.

Also new is a trio of suites paying homage to three different epochs of design: Louis XIV; Louis XV; art deco. The construction and furnishing of the suites have been (just like everything else in the hotel) closely overseen by the owner, Mme Augier. Responsible for much of the outstanding art collection, the architectural imports from ruined chateaus and myriad details right down to a washstand once owned by Napoleon, Mme Augier cares for her hotel as if it were her home. Which, in fact, it is. Resident in the hotel and habitual diner in the Chantecler (you'll notice her favourite cushion plumped up on her seat), she adds a touch of high-brow homeliness to the hotel.

ESSENTIALS

Le Masséna

58 rue Gioffredo (04 92 47 88 88/
www.hotel-massena-nice.com). €€€.
Don't be misled by the stately belle
époque façade of this grand hotel, the
Masséna has its feet firmly planted in
the 21st century. Rooms are smart and
substantial, with all the mod cons you'd
expect for the price, and the bathrooms
are all well proportioned and gleaming.
The vibrant provençal colour scheme of
the lobby extends, in more muted variations, to the rooms themselves, and
even to the seminar and meeting rooms,
which are sunnier and more welcoming
than the featureless norm. Staff, too,
seem to have a breezy and friendly
approach to their work, and are happy
to help with everything from using the
lobby's Wi-Fi connection to organising
a personal car service.

L'Oasis

23 rue Gounod (04 93 88 12 29). €.
A dependable budget option, the cen-
trally located Oasis has been a home
(albeit temporary) to a handful of high-
profile Russian visitors in the past,
most notably Chekhov and Lenin. The
rooms are standard but perfectly comfortable, and the larger ones overlook
a lovely mature garden.

La Petite Sirène

8 rue Maccarani (04 97 03 03 40). €€.
In the enclave of dignified residential
streets surrounding boulevard Victor
Hugo, this appealing, unpretentious
hotel is a quiet, convenient and, above
all, welcoming place to stay. Rooms are
not going to win any design awards but
are more than adequate for a good
night's kip, and the place has that reas-
suringly clean, efficient and friendly
atmosphere that one always hopes to
find in a home away from home.

Le Roosevelt

16 rue Maréchal Joffre (04 93 87 94
71/www.comfort-hotel-nice.com). €€.
It may not be the most glamorous hotel
in this part of town but the Roosevelt
offers comfort and convenience to those
who are not going to be disappointed

by the absence of boutique-style furnishings. What the Roosevelt does have
is a good choice of quiet, cosy guest
rooms, some with balconies, some overlooking the sleepy courtyard at the
back, and all with direct phone lines
and Wi-Fi capability. Staff are friendly
and knowledgeable about their city.

Le Splendid

50 boulevard Victor Hugo (04 93 16
41 00/www.splendid-nice.com). €€€.
Now in its third generation of owner-
ship by the same family, the Splendid
may not be able to offer much in the
way of architectural charm (at least, not
compared to many of the city's other
four-stars) but it certainly makes up for
it in terms of comfort, location, and, its
most famous asset, a superb rooftop
pool. Rooms are spacious, and some (at
the top of the range) have balconies.

La Villa Victoria

33 boulevard Victor Hugo (04 93 88
39 60/www.villa-victoria.com). €€.
The main attraction of this comfortably renovated belle époque villa is its
beautiful *jardin botanique*, featuring all
kinds of specimen plants and trees
from the region, as well as a wonderfully romantic rose pergola – the perfect spot to escape the sun for a quiet
siesta or an intimate, whispered conversation. Failing that, you can confine
your sleeping to the spacious, if rather
flowery, rooms.

Le Wilson

39 rue de l'Hôtel des Postes (04 93 85
47 79/www.hotel-wilson-nice.com). €.
There are many reasons why people
choose to come back to this charming
budget hotel. The room rates (some of
the very cheapest that can be found
anywhere in Nice) are of course one,
but so too are the kookily decorated
rooms (themed on Asia or Africa, or the
work of artists ranging from Dalí to
Matisse), the infectiously upbeat host
and his lovely dining room, enlivened
by homely touches and the convivial
chat of the guests. As the hotel's liter-
ature proudly declares, you'll be sleeping under a beautiful star.

HI Hôtel p136

Le Windsor

*11 rue Dalpozzo (04 93 88 59 35/
www.hotelwindsornice.com). €€.*
Beloved of the arty crowd, the Windsor
has to be the most boho-chic hotel in
Nice. Its mission: to incorporate contemporary art into the decor not only of its
rooms but of its public spaces too (the
mural of a space rocket in the lift is quite
an eye-catcher). Whether you choose to
accept it or not is up to you, but if you
do, make sure you check in to one of the
25 artist-decorated rooms. Work is by
Olivier Mosset, Noël Dolla and
Basserode, among many others. The
remaining rooms, which have not been
decked out by a named artist (that's
about half of them), feature frescoes or
giant posters instead. There's also a
very stylish, very Zen fitness suite with
a hammam and sauna, into which you
can retreat should you suddenly feel
your senses have been over-stimulated.

Promenade & Beaches

Albert 1er

*4 avenue des Phocéens (04 93 85 74
01/www.hotel-albert-1er.com). €€.*
Overlooking the gardens of the same
name, this attractive belle époque hotel
continues to beguile guests with its
low-key brand of old-world charm.
Rooms containing antique armoires
and oak bedsteads are furnished with
elegant restraint, and those facing the
sea are warmed by the sunlight that
streams in through floor-to-ceiling windows. The breakfast room retains
something of the atmosphere of a 1930s
seaside hotel.

Hôtel Park

*6 avenue de Suède (04 97 03 19 00/
www.boscolohotels.com). €€€.*
Owned by Italian luxury hotel chain
Boscolo, the Park is a sophisticated
operation, many of whose rooms overlook the bustling Jardin Albert 1er.
Everything from the stately hush of the
lobby to the discreetly decorated guest
rooms is aimed at smoothing out the
rough edges of travel. There is a restaurant on site but the real pleasure of an

address like this is the chance it offers
you to walk right out into the heart of
Nice for an evening meal and return at
a leisurely stroll.

Mercure Marché aux Fleurs

*91 quai des Etats Unis (04 93 85
74 19/www.mercure.com). €€.*
A link in the Mercure hotel chain, this
seafront hotel is all about location.
Great views at great prices are the
main attraction, but the attentive,
dynamic service and clean, smart
rooms are appealing extras. A good
base, then, but not somewhere you'll
find yourself wanting to linger all day.

Le Negresco

*37 promenade des Anglais (04 93 16
64 00/www.hotel-negresco-nice.com).
€€€€.*
See box p137.

Le Palais de la Méditerranée

*13-15 promenade des Anglais (04 92
14 77 00/www.concorde-hotels.com).
€€€€.*
After a roaring debut in the 1920s, the
Palais de la Med (like many of its
louche aristocratic patrons of the era)
underwent a period of inexorable
decline until its eventual demolition in
the late '70s. Only its iconic (and listed)
art deco façade was preserved, and it
is within this historic shell that the
Concorde group has inserted a thoroughly modern, luxurious hotel. As
you might expect from the prom-front
location, the sea views here are extraordinary, both from the guestrooms
(though not all of them) and from the
public spaces, notably the beautiful
pool on the third floor. Locally inspired
haute cuisine comes by courtesy of talented chef Philippe Thomas in the
hotel's Le Padouk restaurant.

Port & Around

Comfort Hotel Nice Vieux Port

*8 rue Emmanuel Philibert (04 93 31
14 35). €€.*

ESSENTIALS

Cannes .... Autrement

Live Cannes differently

Special offers "Time Out" readers

Upon presentation of this guide, **one extra night offered**

for each stay of minimum 5 nights either at Cavendish or at Villa Garbo

 Package 5 nights Cavendish
as from

 Package 5 nights Villa Garbo
as from

Tél. : +33 (0)4 97 06 26 00
www.cavendish-cannes.com

Tél. : +33 (0)4 93 46 66 00
www.villagarbo-cannes.com

prior reservation requested

One of the few hotels on the harbour side of the Colline, the Comfort offers clean, simple and convenient accommodation at affordable prices. Staying here also means it's a good deal easier to just drift out of the door of an evening to have a quayside aperitif or just sit on the dock of the bay and, er, watch the yachts roll away.

Le Genève

1 rue Cassini (04 93 56 73 73). €.
There are 15 comfortable rooms in this basic but friendly hotel at the place Garibaldi end of rue Cassini. The restaurant, serving traditional French cuisine supplemented by a range of pizzas and salads, is worth a try, should you not have the energy to venture into town.

Kyriad Hôtel

6 rue Emmanuel Philibert (04 93 55 80 00/www.hoteliereduphare.fr). €€.
Just a short walk away from the boat-watching of the portside cafés, this straightforward chain hotel doesn't pretend to offer anything more than a clean and comfortable room for the night, with a few mod cons thrown in. And what it does, it does very well, with helpful and affable staff ensuring the whole operation runs smoothly.

Cimiez & Neighbourhood Nice

Le Floride

52 boulevard de Cimiez (04 93 53 11 02/www.hotel-floride.fr). €.
One of the best-value hotels in town (well, not quite in town, but just a 15-minute walk away), the Floride is a place to dump your bags, eat your meals and crash for the night. In other words, the decor is modest and, while it has a kind of kitsch charm of its own, this is probably not going to be somewhere you'll want to hang out for long periods of time. If you're in town to see the sights, hit the bars and restaurants, and spend your time out and about, then this is the hotel for you. But if it's a pampering break in the sun you'd set your heart on, check in somewhere else.

Le Negresco p141

Hôtel du Petit Palais

17 avenue Emile Bieckiert (04 93 62 19 11/www.petitpalaisnice.com). €.
In keeping with the splendour of its location among the mansions of Cimiez, this small (25-room) but characterful belle époque hotel has plenty to recommend it to the visitor. Many of the original features have been retained and the resultant mood of the lobby and guest-rooms is, as with so many of the aspects of the buildings in this bewitching neighbourhood, one of belonging to a lost but more glamorous era. Although it's only a short distance from the town, the Petit Palais has a sense of glorious isolation (especially on a sunny day, when the hilltop views of Nice and its coastline are quite sensational). Even now, it's easy to see

ESSENTIALS

what prompted playwright and film director Sacha Guitry to lodge here during his spell in Nice in the 1930s.

Trip: Cannes

Le Carlton

58 La Croisette (04 93 06 40 06/ www.ichotelsgroup.com). €€€€.

Probably the most famous hotel in Cannes, the Carlton is surrounded by a golden haze of glamour and high-rolling history. It's still the top choice for film festival purists, although some of the big players have, in recent years, been lured away by the Hôtel du Cap Eden-Roc, an exclusive hideaway a few miles up the coast. A seemingly endless motorcade of expensive cars seems to pull up outside the Carlton's iconic façade (legend has it that architect Charles Dalmas modelled its two *coupoles* on the breasts of the famous gypsy courtesan la Belle Otéro), delivering guests into the care of the attentive, professional staff. Deluxe rooms have incredible views of the bay and the mountains beyond, bettered only by the top-floor suites. The hotel's brasserie delivers fine food at sane prices, and if you're lucky, the odd glimpse of a tuxed-up movie star.

Le Cavendish

11 boulevard Carnot (04 97 06 26 00/ www.cavendish-cannes.com). Closed mid Dec-mid Jan. €€€.

Renowned French designer Christophe Tollemer has done a fine job on the interior of this stylish boutique hotel by retaining much of the character of its former incarnation (as the Riviera residence of Lord Henry Cavendish) while managing to fold in all the trappings of a four-star, 21st-century hotel. The building's original belle époque façade remains, as do the art deco lift and the Carrera marble staircase, and a sense of old-world charm is present in every detail, from the antiques in the lounge to the crystal decanters in the bar. The 35 rooms are all beautifully furnished (such as the *'chambre rotonde'* with its parquet flooring and

immaculate bathroom bathed in light), while standard services range from the high-tech (in-room Wi-Fi) to the old-school (lavender water turndown service). Go on, treat yourself.

Château de la Tour

10 avenue Font-de-Veyre (04 93 90 52 52/www.hotelchateaudelatour.com). Closed Jan. €€€.

On the town's outskirts, this converted chateau has all the glamour of the hotels on the Croisette (albeit in a more country-house kind of way) and yet is refreshingly free of the whiff of bling and celeb snobbery that seems to cling to its seaside counterparts. Formal gardens, secluded terraces with wrought-iron railings, and a gorgeous pool looking across a sweeping lawn towards the sea are the first impressions upon arrival, which is more than matched by the artfully subdued splendour of the interior. Muted wallpaper and grand bedsteads give guestrooms an aristocratic feel, while the restaurant, bar and well-stocked cellar perpetuate the sense of having been invited to an upper-class sojourn on the Riviera.

Le Festival

3 rue Molière (04 97 06 64 40/ www.hotel-festival.com). €.

Run by an enthusiastic couple, the Festival is a good bet for straightforward town-centre accommodation. Rooms are well looked after, and some of them overlook the neighbouring orange trees and palms. A small spa (containing a sauna and whirlpool bath) is on hand to keep you nice and relaxed, and the hearty breakfast will ensure you don't go hungry. All in all, the Embassy is a friendly, good-value option.

Hôtel 3.14

5 rue François Einesy (04 92 99 72 00/ www.3-14hotel.com). €€€.

Design is king at this modern, quirky boutique hotel. Each floor is themed to tie in loosely with the design aesthetics of a given continent: Asia is Zen, clean and contained; America is colourful, trashy and pop arty; Africa is filled with dark wood and rich fabrics;

Le Paiais de la Méditerranée p141

Europe is *Moulin Rouge* come to life; and Oceania is like a beach turned to furniture. Great fun, then, and not at the expense of comfort or convenience either. Products, fabrics and fittings are of the highest quality, and in-room broadband, Wi-Fi, flat-screen television and DVD player means only the hyperactive are at risk of boredom. The hotel's private beach takes its design mission right down to the water's edge, sporting a funky turquoise restaurant with bubble barstools and swaying white curtains, and a phalanx of stylish sun-loungers to ensure that even flopping out in the sun and reading an airport paperback looks cool.

Hôtel Embassy
6 rue de Bône (04 97 06 99 00/ www.embassy-cannes.com). €€.
A good central option, the Embassy is a peaceful place to lay your head without having to stray too far from the thick of the action. Rooms are surprisingly spacious and well equipped (Wi-Fi access, flat-screen television) for the price, and the hotel's garden and rooftop pool are convenient oases if you simply want to pad from bed to sunshine and read the morning paper.

Hôtel Molière
5-7 rue Molière (04 93 38 16 16/ www.hotel-moliere.com). €.
Not every hotel in Cannes costs an arm and a leg, and indeed some, like the Molière, are as affordable as you'll find anywhere on the Riviera. Of course, the flip side of the equation is that no one's going to be creeping into your room to plump up the pillows and rearrange your toiletries every time you pop out for a walk, but then, for some people, that probably comes as good news. No frills, then, and no worse off for it, the Molière provides a room for the night (expect pale provençal colours and pretty tiled bathrooms), a charming garden and friendly, switched-on staff. Unsurprisingly, it's a top choice with journalists and film critics come festival time, so be sure to book in advance if you're coming for the flicks.

Hôtel Oxford
148 boulevard de la République (04 93 68 40 83/www.oxfordhotel.fr). €.
It may be a bit of a hike from the Croisette, but this delightful 11-room villa is outstandingly good value. Completely refurbished in 2007, the rooms are clean, comfortable and more stylish than most in this price range (elegant grey walls, claret-coloured bedspreads, discreetly mounted flat-screen televisions). There's also a cool and lush Mediterranean garden, and a decent restaurant on the premises (breakfast on the pretty, shaded terrace costs €6.50).

Majestic Barrière
10 La Croisette (04 92 98 77 00/ www.lucienbarriere.com). Closed mid Nov-Dec. €€€€.
The new kid on the palace hotel block, the Majestic Barrière courts the hip among the blue chip, but before you go booking a room, a quick date for the Blackberry: the hotel will remain closed until March 2008, as part of an extensive series of refurbishments. Changes to decor notwithstanding, accommodation here is of the slick, modern variety, with standard (or 'classique') rooms looking over towards the town, and everything from a superior room upwards facing the turquoise expanse of the Med. A private beach, a sophisticated pool (which will be off-limits due to the refurb until 2009), a pampering health and beauty centre, and a competition-standard tennis club ensure that no guest's leisure requirements are overlooked. It all comes at a price, of course, but for most of the guests here, that's presumably not an issue. And if it is, there's always the chance to win some of it back at the hotel's Les Princes gaming tables.

Le Martinez
73 La Croisette (04 92 98 73 00/ www.hotel-martinez.com). €€€€.
Many a Ralph Lauren suitcase has been unloaded from the porter's trolley at this venerable palace hotel. The iconic white façade remains unchanged since the Martinez's interwar heyday, thanks

ESSENTIALS

Eat in

Sleep, drink and dine under one roof.

Le Carlton

Gyms, spas, pools and fitness suites are all very nice, but surely the greatest luxury of all is to stay in a hotel where some of the best eating and drinking in the city is to be found just a couple of floors below your room. And fortunately for visitors, local hoteliers have been investing a lot of cash towards creating in-house bars and eateries that will make guests think twice before venturing out.

Chief among the recent arrivals is the **Hi Hôtel** (p136), where residents are given top-to-bottom incentives to stay in. A slick rooftop bar matches an upbeat housey soundtrack with open-air *apéros*, while the ground floor and courtyard are home to hip organic restaurant, Cantine Bio d'Alain Alexanian, and one of the most progressive bars in town, billing regular slots from interesting local and visiting DJs. On a similarly stylish trip is the Mahatma restaurant in **Hôtel 3.14** (p144), whose design-conscious decor (plenty of Murano glass and

discreet lighting effects that change by the hour) is the backdrop for spicily exotic cooking. Meanwhile at the bar, Jojo the mixologist from Martinique will keep them coming until you're ready to hit the hay.

But if it's proper old-school glamour you're looking for, then check in at one of the big-hitting addresses on the Croisette. The **Martinez** (p147) has a new chef on the block, who is doing his bit to ensure that every meal of the day for guests is a good one, but purists will tell you that it's the hotel's Amiral Bar that is the real style mecca. With barstools that have been dented by many of the sexiest and wealthiest buttocks in the world, it remains one of the two most sophisticated watering-holes around these parts.

And the other? That's the Bar des Célébrités at the **Carlton** (p144), of course. Sip a cocktail here, or tuck into the menu at the hotel's brasserie, and watch the world drift enviously by.

to the loving attention of its owners, the Taittinger family, and now a revamp of the swanky guestrooms has put the hotel back on the radar of the Riviera's blue-chip clientele. The lobby and entrance also got a shot in the arm a few years ago, as did Zplage, the hotel's private beach, and now the largest on the Croisette. The hotel's decor is themed loosely around the works of the great French designers of the 1930s and '40s, and guestrooms are furnished in warm, soft hues, some of them with extraordinary balconies (the teak terraces attached to the junior suites are beautiful enough to be a film set). The Palme d'Or restaurant is still the culinary seat of Christian Willer, who remains one of the most respected chefs in town. But, as with everything else here, expect to pay for what you get.

Le Mondial

77 rue d'Antibes (04 93 68 70 00/ www.hotelmondial.activehotels.com). €€.
Part of the Best Western chain, the Mondial has a stab at preserving some of the spirit of its art deco premises, but its best feature is its central location and commanding south-facing aspect (plenty of daylight in your room, in other words). Rooms are soundproofed and perfectly comfortable, and some have tiny balconies just about big enough to swing a cat. On which note: pets are allowed.

Le Renoir

7 rue Edith Cavell (04 92 99 62 62/ www.hotel-renoir-cannes.com). €€.
Looking smart and thoroughly modern after a recent makeover, the Renoir has large, well-appointed guest rooms (flat-screen satellite TV, Wi-Fi access), secure parking, and willing and competent staff. The business suites (separate work stations, high-speed internet) are also worth knowing about if you're in town to work.

Sofitel Cannes Le Méditerranée

1 boulevard Jean Hibert (04 92 99 73 00/www.sofitel.com). €€€.

Its enviable location on the mini peninsula that is boulevard Jean Hibert affords Le Méditerranée spectacular views of the bay and the Iles de Lérins in the distance. A secluded rooftop pool makes the most of the panorama, as do the sea-facing rooms. On all other points, this comfortable retreat offers the range of amenities and services associated with the Sofitel brand, including in-room Wi-Fi access and ultra-supportive Mybed mattresses. A new thalassotherapy spa is scheduled to open early in 2009.

Le Splendid

4-6 rue Félix Faure (04 97 06 22 22/ www.splendid-hotel-cannes.fr). €€€.
An historic landmark and justifiably proud of its status as the original palace hotel, the Splendid still looks as if it has been freshly transported from the heady winter seasons of the belle époque. Its wedding cake façade and proud row of fluttering flags is a sepia photograph brought to life and inside, the decor has a similar sense of a past golden age preserved like a fly in amber. Grand brass bedsteads, ornate cast-iron radiators and intricately tiled bathrooms cast a charming veneer over what is otherwise polished, bang up-to-date accommodation with broadband access and satellite television. And if you get the chance, a Splendid balcony breakfast in the morning sunshine is one of the better ways to start a day.

La Villa d'Estelle

14 rue des Belges (04 92 98 44 48/ www.villadestelle.com). €€€€.
This sumptuously appointed, elegant townhouse feels more intimate than your average city-centre hotel. Rooms are beautifully furnished and come equipped with all the latest gadgets, while the apartments and studios are equally sophisticated self-catering options for those coming to Nice on longer visits. There's an attractive pool, an enthusiastic and indulgent workforce, and those myriad little touches that serve to remind you that you are in a seriously swanky joint.

ESSENTIALS

Getting Around

Arriving & leaving

By air

Many low-cost airlines fly regularly to Nice.

Air France *UK 0845 142 4343/USA 1-800 237 2747/France 08 20 82 08 20/www.airfrance.com.* Paris to Nice.
British Airways *UK 0870 850 9850/US 1-800 247 9297/France 08 25 82 54 00/www.britishairways.com.* London Heathrow, Gatwick and Birmingham to Nice.
British Midland *UK 0870 607 0555/France 01 48 62 55 65/www.flybmi.com.* Heathrow and Nottingham to Nice.
Easyjet *UK 0870 600 0000/France 08 25 08 25 08/www.easyjet.com.* Gatwick, Stansted, Aberdeen, Bristol, Liverpool and Luton to Nice.

From the USA, most flights involve a Paris connection.

Delta *US 1-800 241 4141/France 08 00 35 40 80/www.delta.com.* Daily from New York JFK to Nice.

Aéroport Nice-Côte d'Azur

08 20 42 33 33/www.nice.aeroport.fr France's second airport, located 7km (4 miles) west of the centre of Nice. Most airlines use Terminal 1; Air France flights use Terminal 2.

Airport connections

Ligne d'Azur operates a reliable, regular service into town from the airport.

No.98 Nice Direct *Departs Terminals 1 & 2 every 20 mins (6am-11.50pm Mon-Sat).* Regular stops along the Promenade des Anglais and at designated hotels.
Airport **taxis** (04 93 13 78 78) operate 24 hours a day. Onward local helicopter connections are also available through Nice Hélicoptère (04 93 21 34 32).

By rail

The French TGV (high-speed train) runs to the South from Paris Gare de Lyon and Lille, via Lyon, to Avignon. There it splits west to Nîmes and east to Nice via Cannes and Antibes (not all trains stop at all stations). Note that the highest-speed track currently only reaches Marseille and Nîmes.

It takes around 5hrs 30mins to Nice. On slower, long-distance trains from Menton and Nice, you can travel overnight by *couchette* (a bunk-bed sleeping car, shared with up to five others) or *voiture-lit* (a comfier sleeping compartment for up to three). Both are available in first- and second-class, and must be reserved ahead.

You can buy **tickets** in all SNCF stations from counters or by French-issued credit card at automatic ticket machines, also from some travel agents. Phone bookings can be made on 3635 or 08 92 35 35 35 (7am-10pm daily). Bookings can be made online at www.sncf.com and www.tgv.com, and paid online or at ticket machines; certain tickets can be printed out directly at home. The TGV can be booked up to two months ahead; you always have to reserve seats to travel on the TGV.

For all train journeys you must *composter votre billet* – that is, date-stamp your ticket in the orange *composteur* machine on the platform before you start the journey.

SNCF Nice

Station, avenue Thiers (08 92 35 35 35). Ticket office, 2 rue de la Liberté (08 92 35 35 35). **Open** *Tickets* 9.30am-6.30pm Mon-Sat.

By bus

The coastal area between Nice and Cannes is well served by buses.

Eurolines *5 boulevard Jean-Jaurès (04 93 80 08 70).*
Gare Routière *5 boulevard Jean-Jaurès (08 92 70 12 06).*
Phocéens Cars *2 place Masséna (04 93 85 66 61).*

By road

Much of Europe heads south during July and August. Coast roads and motorways crawl at snail's pace, especially between Cannes and Menton. Roads are at their worst on Saturdays and around the 14 July and 15 August public holidays. Look for BIS (*Bison Futé*) signs, which attempt to reduce summer traffic by suggesting diversions.

The distance from Calais to Nice is 1,167km (725 miles); from Caen to Nice 1,161km (721 miles). French autoroutes are toll (*péage*) roads, although some sections – especially around major cities – are free. At *péage* toll-booths, payment can be made by cash or credit card. From Nice airport to Monaco, expect to pay €3.20, and €14 from Aix-en-Provence to Nice.

In normal conditions, speed limits are 130kph (80mph) on autoroutes, 110kph (69mph) on dual carriageways and 90kph (56mph) on other roads.

In heavy rain and fog, these limits are reduced by 20kph (12mph) on autoroutes, 10kph (6mph) on other roads; limits are also reduced during heavy air pollution. The limit in built-up areas is 50kph (28mph), 30kph (17mph) in some districts. Automatic radars have been installed all over France since 2003, which can automatically send off a speeding fine for breaking the speed limit by as little as 6kph.

Car hire

To hire a car you must normally be 25 or over and have held a licence for at least a year. Some hire companies will accept drivers aged 21-24, but a supplement of €8-€15 per day is usual. Remember to bring your driver's licence and passport with you.

Avis *Aéroport Nice-Côte d'Azur, Terminals 1 & 2 (93 21 36 33).*
Europcar *Aéroport Nice-Côte d'Azur, Terminals 1 & 2 (08 25 81 00 81).*
Hertz *9 avenue Thiers (04 97 03 01 20).*

City transport

Bus

Lignes d'Azur
10 avenue Félix Faure (08 10 06 10 06). **Open** 7.15am-7pm Mon-Fri; 8am-6pm Sat).
Operates a full and extensive bus service, including a Noctambus night bus covering four routes and departing every half hour (9.10pm-1.10am) from place Jean-Claude Bermond.

Taxi

Travel by taxi is a luxury in Nice (and Cannes). Note also that night rates operate between 7pm and 7am. The main ranks are at esplanade Masséna, promenade des Anglais, place Garibaldi, rue Hôtel des Postes, SNCF railway station and outside the Acropolis.

Central Riviera Taxi *04 93 13 78 78.*
Cyclo Politain *04 93 81 76 15/www. cyclopolitain.com.* Rickshaws.

Tram

At the time of writing, Nice's new tram system was about to get underway. For details, call 08 11 00 20 06, consult www.tramway nice.org or stop by one of the many green 'Point Infotram' kiosks.

ESSENTIALS

Resources A-Z

Accident & emergency

All EU nationals staying in France are entitled to use the French Social Security system, which refunds up to 70% of medical expenses (but sometimes much less, for example for dental treatment). The old E111 has been replaced by the European Health Insurance Card (EHIC). It is easiest to apply for one online at www.ehicard.org (provide your name, date of birth and NHS or NI number). The E112 form is still valid for those already receiving medical care, such as routine maternity supervision (for further information, see www.dh.gov.uk). Non-EU nationals should take out insurance before leaving home. Fees and prescriptions are paid in full, then reimbursed in part on receipt of a completed *fiche*.

Note that the Sapeurs-Pompiers (fire brigade), who are also trained paramedics, will usually be called out to the scene of accidents rather than the SAMU (ambulance).

Nice Médecins
04 93 52 42 42.

Centre Hospitalier de Cannes
15 avenue Broussailles, Cannes (04 93 69 70 00/www.hopital-canne.fr).

Hôpital Saint Roch
5 rue Pierre Dévoluy, Nice (04 92 03 77 77/www.chu-nice.fr).

Emergency numbers

Ambulance service (SAMU) **15**
Emergencies when calling from a mobile phone **112**
Fire and rescue service (Sapeurs-Pompiers) **18**
Police service **17**

Climate

The weather in Nice is consistently hot and dry, with an average daytime January low temperature of 13°C (55°F). Spring sometimes sees heavy rainfall and November can be blustery and cold, but even then you're likely to get good days in between the bad. Temperatures in the summer can get very high, although the August average maximum is 27°C (81°F). However, it's not unknown for the thermometer to climb above 38°C (100°F). The best advice then is to stay in the shade and to drink plenty of water.

Credit card loss

In case of credit card loss or theft, call one of the following 24hr services which have English-speaking staff:
American Express 01 47 77 72 00
Diners Club 08 20 00 07 34
MasterCard 01 45 67 84 84
Visa 08 92 70 57 05

Customs

There are no limits on the quantity of goods you can take into France from another EU country for personal use, provided tax has been paid in the country of origin. Beware bringing in fake designer goods from the markets at Ventimiglia and San Remo: the goods may be confiscated and you might have to pay a fine. Personal limits are:

- up to 800 cigarettes, 400 small cigars, 200 cigars or 1kg loose tobacco.
- 10 litres of spirits (over 22% alcohol), 90 litres of wine (under 22% alcohol) or 110 litres of beer.

For goods from outside the EU:

- 200 cigarettes or 100 small cigars, 50 cigars or 250g loose tobacco.
- 1 litre of spirits (over 22% alcohol) and 2 litres of wine (under 22% alcohol) and beer.
- 50g perfume.

Visitors can carry up to €7,600 in currency.

Tax refunds (détaxe)

Non-EU residents can claim a refund on VAT (TVA) on some items if they spend over €175 in one day. Ask for a *bordereau de vente à l'exportation* form in the shop and when you leave France have it stamped by Customs; then post the form back to the shop.

Dental emergency

Refunds of medical expenses for dental treatment may not always be covered to the same extent (that is, up to 70%) as they are with other areas of medicine.

Dental emergencies

Hôpital Saint Roch, Nice (04 92 03 33 33).

SOS Dentaire

Cannes (04 93 68 28 00).

Disabled

Travel & transport

Taxi drivers cannot legally refuse to take disabled people or guide dogs, and must help them get into the taxi.

SNCF runs train carriages designed to accommodate

wheelchairs. For information, call 08 00 15 47 53. People accompanying handicapped passengers get free travel or reductions, as do guide dogs.

Location de Véhicules Equipés et Automatiques

51 rue Celony, 13100 Aix-en-Provence (04 42 93 54 59/www.lvea.fr). The nearest rental facility for specially adapted cars for disabled drivers; around €100/day.

Eurotunnel

03 21 00 61 00/UK 0870 535 3535/ www.eurotunnel.com. The Channel Tunnel car-on-a-train is good for disabled passengers; you may stay in your vehicle and get a 10% discount as well.

Groupement pour Insertion des Handicapés Physiques (GIHP)

04 91 11 41 00. Information on disabled transport.

Holidays & accommodation

Tourist offices should be able to provide information on sights and hotels accessible to the disabled. Disabled parking is indicated with a blue wheelchair sign; the international orange disabled parking disc is also recognised. To hire a wheelchair or other equipment, enquire at the local pharmacy. In Nice, part of the public beach has been adapted for wheelchairs with ramp access and a concrete platform.

Gîtes Accessibles à Tous (Gîtes de France, 59 rue St-Lazare, 75009 Paris, 01 49 70 75 85, www.gites-de-france.fr) lists holiday rentals equipped for the disabled. The *French Federation of Camping and Caravanning Guide* and the *Michelin Green Guide – Camping/ Caravanning France* both list campsites with disabled facilities.

ESSENTIALS

Useful addresses

Association des Paralysés de France

01 40 78 69 00.

RADAR (Royal Association for Disability & Rehabilitation)

Unit 12, City Forum, 250 City Road, London EC1V 8AF (7250 3222/ www.radar.org.uk).

Drugs

Possession of drugs is illegal in France. Possession of even a small amount of cannabis for personal use could land you in jail and incur a large fine.

Electricity

Electricity in France runs on 220V, so visitors with British 240V appliances can use a converter (*adaptateur*), which you'll find for sale at hardware shops. For American 110V appliances, you will need a transformer (*transformateur*), available at FNAC and Darty chains.

Embassies & consulates

For general enquiries, passports or visas, you usually need to go to your consulate rather than your embassy. A full list of embassies and consulates appears in *Pages Jaunes* under 'Ambassades et Consulats' (or alternatively see www.pagesjaunes.fr).

Consulates in and around Nice & Cannes

Canada

10 rue Lamartine, 06000 Nice (04 93 92 93 22).

Republic of Ireland

152 boulevard JF Kennedy, 06160 Cap d'Antibes (04 93 61 50 63).

United Kingdom

24 avenue du Prado, 13006 Marseille (04 91 15 72 10).

United States

7 ave Gustave V, 06000 Nice (04 93 88 89 55).

Embassies in Paris

Australia

01 40 59 33 00/ www.france.embassy.gov.au.

Canada

01 44 43 29 00/ www.amb-canada.fr.

New Zealand

01 45 01 43 43/ www.nzembassy.com/france.

Republic of Ireland

01 44 17 67 00.

Republic of South Africa

01 53 59 23 23/ www.afriquesud.net.

United Kingdom

01 44 51 31 00/www.amb-grandebretagne.fr.

United States

01 43 12 22 22/www.amb-usa.fr.

Internet

The high numbers of tourists visiting the city means that there are a great many internet cafés and phone/internet stations to choose from in Vieux Nice. Cannes, too, has more than its fair share, so you should never have to travel far before going online. The two we have listed below are particularly friendly and proficient, and are convivial meeting points for travellers and ex-pats.

Email Café

8 rue Saint Vincent, Nice (04 93 62 68 86). **Open** 9am-7pm Mon-Sat.

Webcenter

26 rue Hoche, Cannes (04 93 68 72 37). **Open** 10am-11pm Mon-Sat; noon-8pm Sun.

Opening hours

Shops are generally open between 9.30am and 7pm, although food shops tend to open earlier. The sacred lunch hour is still largely observed, which means that many shops and offices close at noon or 1pm and reopen at 2pm or later. Many shops also close for the morning or all day on Monday. Hypermarkets (*grandes surfaces*) usually stay open throughout lunchtime. Most shops close on Sundays, though *bureaux de tabac* (which sell stamps as well as cigarettes) and newsagents are often open Sunday mornings, and *boulangeries* (bakers) may be open every day.

Public offices and *mairies* (town halls) usually open 8.30am-noon, then 2-6pm. Many museums close for lunch; they also close on certain public holidays, notably 1 Jan, 1 May and 25 Dec. National museums usually close on Tuesday.

French banks usually open 9am-5pm Monday to Friday (some close at lunch); some banks also open on Saturday. All are closed on public holidays, and from noon on the previous day.

Police

Police in urban and rural areas come under two different governmental organisations. The **Gendarmerie nationale** is a military force serving under the Ministère de la Défense and its network covers minor towns and rural areas. The **Police nationale** serve under the Ministère de l'Intérieur in main cities.

Beware of car crime. Police advise leaving nothing visible in parked cars. In Nice there has also been a spate of car jackings – car theft as people are parking.

If you are robbed, you need to make a statement at the police station or gendarmerie for your insurance claim.

Commissariat de Cannes

1 avenue de Grasse, Cannes (04 93 06 22 22). **Open** 24hrs daily.

Commissariat de Nice

1 avenue Maréchal Foch (04 92 17 22 22). **Open** 24hrs daily.

Post

Postes (post offices) are usually open 9am-noon and 2-7pm Monday to Friday, and 9am-noon on Saturday. In main post offices, individual counters are marked according to the services they provide; if you just need stamps, go to the window marked '*Timbres*'.

If you need to send an urgent letter or parcel overseas, ask for it to be sent through **Chronopost**, which is faster but more expensive. Chronopost is also fastest for parcels within France; packages up to 25kg are guaranteed to be delivered within 24hrs.

For a small fee, you can arrange for mail to be kept *poste restante*, addressed to Poste Restante, Poste Centrale (for main post office), then the town postcode and name. You will need to present your passport when collecting mail.

Stamps are also available at tobacconists (*bureaux de tabac*) and other shops selling postcards and greetings cards. For standard-weight letters or postcards (up to 20g within France and 10g within the EU) a 50¢ stamp is needed.

Telegrams can be sent during *poste* hours or by phone (24hr); to send a telegram abroad, dial 08 00 33 44 11.

Smoking

Despite health campaigns and a law that insists restaurants provide non-smoking areas (*zones non-fumeurs*), the French remain enthusiastic smokers. Cigarettes are officially only on sale in *tabacs*, which tend to close at 8pm, and 2pm on Sundays.

Telephones

Telephone numbers are always ten figures, written in sets of two, eg 01 23 45 67 89. If you want numbers to be given singly rather than in pairs as is customary, ask for *chiffre par chiffre*. Regional telephone numbers are prefixed as follows: Paris & Ile de France 01; North-west 02; North-east 03; South-east and Corsica 04; and South-west 05. Mobile phones start 06. When calling from abroad, omit the zero. The code for dialling France is 33; for Monaco it is 377.

Public phones

Public phone boxes use phone cards (*télécartes*),which are available from post offices, stationers, stations, *tabacs* and some cafés. To make a call from a public phone box, lift the receiver, insert the card, then dial the number. To make a follow-on call, do not replace the receiver but press the green '*appel suivant*' button and dial.

International calls

Dial 00 followed by the country's international code.
Australia 00 61
Canada 00 1

Ireland 00 353
Monaco 00 377
New Zealand 00 64
South Africa 00 27
UK 00 44
USA 00 1

Special rates

In France telephone numbers that start with the following prefixes are charged at special rates:

0800 Numéro vert Freephone.
0801 Numéro azur 11¢ first 3mins, then 4¢/min.
0802 Numéro indigo I 15¢/min.
0803 Numéro indigo II 23¢/min.
0867 23¢/min.
0836/0868/0869 34¢/min.

Mobile phones

France has just three mobile phone operators, offering a sometimes confusing array of subscriptions and prepaid card systems. The operators are Bouygues, France Telecom/Orange and SFR.

Misterrent

www.misterrent.com
This internet-based company will work out which of its nationwide network of outlet franchises is nearest to you, then bike a phone to you from there.

Rentacell

08.10.00.00.92/www.rentacell.com
Rentacell offers mobile phone rental for €8/day or €30/wk; calls within France cost 76¢/min, international calls cost €1.22/min, and incoming calls are free. There's same-day delivery to your hotel or an airport if you're staying in Cannes or Nice.

Phone directories

Phone directories can be found in all post offices and in most cafés. The *Pages Blanches* provides a listing of people and businesses in alphabetical order. *Pages Jaunes*

ESSENTIALS

lists businesses and services by category. Both are available on www.pagesjaunes.fr.

24-hour services

French directory enquiries (renseignements) 12.
International directory enquiries 32 12 then country code (eg 44 for UK, 1 for USA).
Telephone engineer 13.
International news (French recorded message, France Inter) 08 36 68 10 33 (34¢/min).
To send a telegram (all languages): international 08 00 33 44 11, within France 36 55.
Speaking clock 36 99.

Tickets

The best starting point for buying tickets in Nice is either direct from the venue itself or online at www.ticketnet.fr. Cannes is a similar story, with the additional resource of the Palais des Festivals et Congrès, which has a ticket office inside the Cannes Tourist Office (see below).

Time

France is one hour ahead of Greenwich Mean Time (GMT) and six hours ahead of New York. The clocks change between summer and winter time on the same date as the UK. The 24hr clock is frequently used in France when giving times: 8am is *huit heures*, noon (*midi*) is *douze heures*, 8pm is *vingt heures* and midnight (*minuit*) is *zéro heure*.

Tipping

By law a service charge of 10-15% is included in the bill in all restaurants; leave a small extra tip of 50¢-€2 on the table if you are particularly pleased. In taxis, round

up to the nearest 50¢ or €1; give €1-€2 to porters, doormen, hairdressers and guides. In a bar or café, just leave small change.

Tourist information

Cannes Tourist Office
Esplanade Georges Pompidou (04 92 99 84 22/www.cannes-on-line.com). **Open** *Sept-June* 9am-7pm daily. *July, Aug* 9am-8pm daily.

Nice Tourist Office
5 promenade des Anglais (08 92 70 74 07/www.nicetourism.com). **Open** 8am-8pm Mon-Sat; 9am-7pm Sun.

What's on

The first resource for information on events, festivals and concerts in Nice and Cannes should be the respective tourist offices, which publish seasonal magazines and brochures with exhaustive listings. In Nice, for events that may slip under the tourist office radar, try the free *Street Mag*, which is available in bars and shops around Vieux Nice.

Gay events and club nights are often advertised at specific venues, such as Nice's Blue Boy, Le Flag and Le Klub (which also has its own magazine). Alternatively, see the website listings of France Queer Resources Directory at www.france.qrd.org.

Visas

To visit France, you need a valid passport. Non-EU citizens require a visa, although citizens of Australia, Canada, New Zealand and the USA do not need a visa for stays of up to three months. If in any doubt, check with the French consulate in your country. If you intend to stay in France for more than 90 days, then you are supposed to apply for a *carte de séjour*.

Index